NAVAL POSTGRADUATE SCHOOL
Monterey, California

THESIS

ANALYSIS OF FRATRICIDE IN UNITED STATES
NAVAL SURFACE AND SUBMARINE FORCES
IN THE SECOND WORLD WAR

by

Lars R. H. Orloff

September, 1999

Thesis Advisor: Wayne P. Hughes, Jr.

Approved for public release; distribution is unlimited.

20000306 040

REPORT DOCUMENTATION PAGE

Form Approved
OMB No. 0704-0188

1. AGENCY USE ONLY *(Leave blank)*	2. REPORT DATE September 1999	3. REPORT TYPE AND DATES COVERED Master's Thesis

4. TITLE AND SUBTITLE
Analysis of Fratricide in United States Naval Surface and Submarine Forces in the Second World War

5. FUNDING NUMBERS

6. AUTHOR(S)
Lars R. Hagendorf-Orloff

7. PERFORMING ORGANIZATION NAME(S) AND ADDRESS(ES)
Naval Postgraduate School
Monterey, CA 93943-5000

8. PERFORMING ORGANIZATION REPORT NUMBER

9. SPONSORING / MONITORING AGENCY NAME(S) AND ADDRESS(ES)

10. SPONSORING / MONITORING AGENCY REPORT NUMBER

11. SUPPLEMENTARY NOTES
The views expressed in this thesis are those of the author and do not reflect the official policy or position of the Department of Defense or the U.S. Government.

12a. DISTRIBUTION / AVAILABILITY STATEMENT
Approved for public release; distribution is unlimited.

12b. DISTRIBUTION CODE

13. ABSTRACT *(maximum 200 words)*

Friendly fire in naval warfare is a virtually unstudied phenomenon. In order to prepare future U.S. naval forces for the inevitable losses that will occur as a result of fratricide, we must look to the past to discover the role it has played in this century's wars at sea. This study examines the significance of friendly fire in U.S. naval surface and submarine operations during World War II and argues that the occurrence of self-inflicted casualties is a function primarily of the frequency and intensity of naval combat. Additionally, the causes of and factors contributing to naval fratricide are identified and discussed in detail using historical cases. The crucial result of this thesis is that even the most technologically advanced and highly trained force is subject to surprisingly high rates of friendly fire. Only when the vulnerability of every navy to fratricide is officially acknowledged can technology and doctrine be developed to reduce the risk of accidentally engaging one's own forces.

14. SUBJECT TERMS
Fratricide, U.S. naval forces in World War II.

15. NUMBER OF PAGES
94

16. PRICE CODE

17. SECURITY CLASSIFICATION OF REPORT	18. SECURITY CLASSIFICATION OF THIS PAGE	19. SECURITY CLASSIFI- CATION OF ABSTRACT	20. LIMITATION OF ABSTRACT
Unclassified	Unclassified	Unclassified	UL

NSN 7540-01-280-5500

Standard Form 298 (Rev. 2-89)
Prescribed by ANSI Std. 239-18

ANALYSIS OF FRATRICIDE IN UNITED STATES NAVAL SURFACE AND SUBMARINE FORCES IN THE SECOND WORLD WAR

Lars R. H. Orloff
Lieutenant, United States Navy
B.S., United States Naval Academy, 1993

Submitted in partial fulfillment of the
requirements for the degree of

MASTER OF SCIENCE IN OPERATIONS RESEARCH

from the

NAVAL POSTGRADUATE SCHOOL

September 1999

Author: _____
Lars R. H. Orloff

Approved by: _____
Wayne P. Hughes, Jr., Thesis Advisor

_____
James N. Eagle, Second Reader

_____
Richard E. Rosenthal, Chairman
Department of Operations Research

iii

ABSTRACT

Friendly fire in naval warfare is a virtually
unstudied phenomenon. In order to prepare future U.S.
naval forces for the inevitable losses that will occur as a
result of fratricide, we must look to the past to discover
the role it has played in this century's wars at sea. This
study examines the significance of friendly fire in U.S.
naval surface and submarine operations during World War II
and argues that the occurrence of self-inflicted casualties
is a function primarily of the frequency and intensity of
naval combat. Additionally, the causes of and factors
contributing to naval fratricide are identified and
discussed in detail using historical cases. The crucial
result of this thesis is that even the most technologically
advanced and highly trained force is subject to
surprisingly high rates of friendly fire. Only when the
vulnerability of every navy to fratricide is officially
acknowledged can technology and doctrine be developed to
reduce the risk of accidentally engaging one's own forces.

TABLE OF CONTENTS

ACKNOWLEDGEMENTS

This thesis was made possible because of the contributions of several people. My advisor Wayne Hughes initially gave me the idea and motivation, and he let me run with the project. I thank him primarily for allowing me the freedom to create the study as I saw fit. His expertise in naval history and tactics was of tremendous value as was his faith in my research and writing abilities. I have heard Captain Hughes described by a peer as "a great American," and I believe this truly. My one regret is that I had only a short time to work with him and benefit from his vast experience and infinite knowledge.

Tom Lucas provided invaluable assistance in the statistical sampling, regression, and Poisson applicability portions of this study. I am especially grateful to him because he is not officially a part of the thesis; he offered to help simply because I am a former student of his. In addition to proofreading sections of text, he helped provide a statistical interpretation of the results of the numerous regressions I performed. I greatly appreciate both his interest and the time he spent on this project.

Finally, I would not have been able to accomplish anything in the last two years without the support and patience of my soon-to-be wife Jennifer. I can never repay her tolerance of my countless frustrations with this thesis, schoolwork, projects, exams, and software formatting. Thank you, Jen, for staying with me.

I. INTRODUCTION

A. NEED FOR NAVAL STUDY

> Death and wounding by our own hand in ground
> combat happens far more frequently than is
> officially acknowledged, and current efforts to
> reduce incidents of fratricide on future
> battlefields will remain half-measures until
> historical fact is incorporated into the
> doctrinal base that drives policy. (Hawkins,
> 1994, p. 55)

This introductory paragraph of Charles Hawkins'
outstanding article "Fratricide: Facts, Myths, and
Misperceptions" is the inspiration behind this study.
While the high friendly fire (fratricide) casualty rate of
Operation Desert Storm stimulated a national consciousness
of the subject, the Department of Defense was willing to
explain away the resulting 17% friendly casualty proportion
(of total force casualties) as an anomaly due to the short
duration of the war, the low number of overall personnel
casualties, and the battle inexperience of front line
troops. (Hawkins, 1994, p. 55) This "disingenuous,
bureaucratic mumble" has had the effect of downplaying not
only the role of friendly fire in the Gulf War but also the
significance of fratricide in the history of warfare. As
Hawkins details in his article, historical analyses have
proven that the Desert Storm self-inflicted casualty
percentage is not an aberration. According to several
studies, friendly fire casualty rates of several major
operations in World War II produced proportions that are
higher than 10% and even as great as 24%. (Hawkins, 1994,
p. 57)

1

Research into ground force friendly fire is relatively thorough, and numerous analyses and reports on the subject have been completed. However, only two naval studies are known to exist, both of which were published in 1995. The first is a superb work by Paul Kemp titled *Friend or Foe: Friendly Fire at Sea 1939-1945*. The other, conducted by Eleanor Gauker and Christopher Blood, is an article published in the *Naval War College Review* named "Friendly Fire Incidents during World War II Naval Operations."

Neither study gives significant weight to the causes of fratricide hypothesized by the Department of Defense in the wake of the Persian Gulf War. For example, the Gauker-Blood article groups friendly fire incidents documented in the Naval Historical Division's *United States Naval Chronology, World War II* into occurrences by vessel type and tactical situation. The data surprisingly demonstrate that fully 75% of the war's fratricide incidents occurred in 1945, when front line naval forces had already endured three years of battle. The amount of combat experience does not appear to be a factor, as Gauker and Blood report:

> ...the number of friendly fire incidents increased with the intensity of World War II naval operations. The Okinawa campaign [April-June 1945] alone accounted for twenty-two incidents, or 42 percent of the total for the entire war. (Gauker and Blood, 1995, p. 117)

The article implies that the tactical situation was an important factor in the number of fratricide cases. Of 53 incidents, 25 occurred during amphibious landing and assault operations. These landings were often fiercely opposed and involved the coordination of hundreds of ships, transports, landing craft, and aircraft. Attacks, raids, and sorties (offensive operations conducted by aircraft carrier forces) contributed nine incidents to the total. In contrast, only 3 incidents were the result of naval battle, where the number of involved vessels of any type, in relation to an amphibious assault, was small. (Gauker and Blood, 1995, pp. 117-118)

It is impossible to know how prepared today's American Navy is for the inevitability of self-inflicted losses during combat. World War II was the last major naval war, and today's Navy has yet to be tested in an evenly matched battle. The dependence on computers and Identification Friend or Foe equipment to sort the battlefield may only serve to perpetuate fratricide when the shooting starts. Incidents of fratricide during Desert Storm, the USS Vincennes tragedy, and the destruction of two U.S. Army helicopters by their Air Force comrades in April 1994 continue to remind us of the inability of technology alone to solve identification problems. Technology can help the situation, but only if it is implemented as part of a greater effort to reduce friendly fire. As will be discussed in detail, the solution must include improved operational doctrine and better communication between commands controlling forces that operate in a common area.

The first step in making the necessary changes to operational policy and technology is to acknowledge the role fratricide has played, and will play, in the history of naval warfare. This study serves three primary purposes; it will determine the proportion of friendly fire incidents suffered by U.S. naval forces in World War II, examine the dependence of friendly fire on the intensity of specific types of naval combat, and discuss the nature of naval fratricide and its effect in numerous cases during the war. Only when the truth of the history of fratricide is brought to light can a serious effort be made toward its reduction in future conflicts.

B. HISTORY OF NAVAL FRATRICIDE

When compared to the history of land combat, the accidental engagement of one's own force at sea is a relatively recent hazard for naval commanders. Before the advent of long-range artillery, submarines, and aircraft, naval battles were fought between opponents well within sight of one another. From the early days of the Mediterranean galley to roughly the end of the 16th century, the vessels of rival navies were brought alongside each other and fierce actions were fought by soldiers and sailors using ground combat weapons. Most often, the objective was to board the ship of one's enemy and initiate a hand-to-hand mêlée that would eventually produce a victor. Fratricide took the form of undisciplined pike or sword strokes or the misdirected fire from archers, crossbowmen, and soldiers using primitive gunpowder weapons. Even so, its significance was small because the vessels themselves were not damaged.

The 17th and 18th centuries saw the evolution of the warship and its armament into a unique weapon that, in turn, developed naval combat into an increasingly distinct form of warfare. During the engagement of the Spanish Armada in 1588, English captains realized the effectiveness of standing off with their long-range cannon against their numerically superior enemy. By avoiding grappling and boarding actions with the Spanish galleons, the English deprived them of the effective use of their short barrel, siege-type cannon that were murderous at close range. As a result, long-barreled guns began to dominate the gundecks of warships in the 17th century. Since it was possible to inflict significant damage at increasingly greater range, boarding actions were ever more rare. Speed and mobility became as valuable as effective gunnery; naval architects began to design ships that had optimal sailing qualities in addition to a sufficient number of cannon. The naval battle had become an engagement combining maneuver and gunnery; hence, it existed as a highly specialized and unique type of combat.

As a result, the combat power of the 17th century squadron or fleet was measured by the number of its ships and guns. Thus, the control of any sea region was dependent on the size of the force holding it. The warship, rather than its crew, had become the primary target of an opposing commander desiring to wrest control of an area from his adversary. Consequently, fleet tactics developed around gaining the greatest advantage from the design of each ship. Naval commanders ultimately fought their ships in columns, thus giving their broadside-mounted cannon the most devastating cumulative effect. Engagements became very tightly controlled affairs, as each fleet formed into a "line of battle" preceding the opening shots. Tactics were so strictly enforced and movement so slow that it was not uncommon for each group of ships to maneuver for hours prior to an impending action in order to establish their formations and gain the best wind advantage. The speed of approach of the foes was usually less than ten knots, and their maximum effective range of engagement was not more than half of a nautical mile.

As long as the columns were maintained, misidentification was scarcely possible. Friendly fire generally occurred as a result of the disintegration of a formal battle into a mêlée. Here, cannon fire that missed its intended target could conceivably strike and damage a friendly vessel, especially when ships were obscured by the dense smoke produced by the firing of hundreds of cannon at close quarters. The effect of the misdirected fire would have been minimal, however, since the process by which one could significantly damage, much less sink, another vessel was relatively slow.

The dawn of steam propulsion in the middle of the 19th century allowed ships to sail the world's oceans free of the restraint of the prevailing wind. Battles increasingly were fought by ships that engaged one another from any direction and in any wind condition from a dead calm to a fierce gale. Gun systems had become more powerful and efficient, such that the destructive potential of a single ship with only a fraction of the number of weapons of its predecessors was continually increasing. By the turn of the century, improvements in the range and accuracy of naval artillery had increased engagement distances to the limit of the visual horizon, leading to the ever-greater possibility of mistaking a friend for an enemy.

Sea mines had been in military use for over a hundred years, but their improvement during the First World War demonstrated that they could be employed effectively across stretches of water hundreds of nautical miles wide. An ingenious firing mechanism designed by an American inventor enabled a nearby target to detonate a mine without striking its casing. Other weapons were being developed that would likewise reduce the ability of a force to identify its enemy prior to attack. Submarines, themselves difficult to recognize as such and positively identify, were able to engage a target based solely on its sound. Their straight-running, magnetic, and acoustic torpedoes did not discriminate between German, Japanese, British, or American targets. By 1940, aircraft were flying at speeds in excess of 350 miles-per-hour. Despite colorful markings, they were inherently difficult to identify at any speed, and their presence on the naval battlefield dramatically reduced the reaction time of a ship or submarine to an air attack. Because waiting for positive identification of an approaching plane could be disastrous, ship captains in many cases gave standing orders to gun crews to engage air targets as soon as they were sighted and came in range.

It was inevitable, then, that the nature and complexity of huge armadas of thousands of ships, submarines, and airplanes, each individually deadly, would create in World War II a situation in which fratricide would play a significant role.

II. DISCUSSION

A. THESIS DEFINITION OF FRATRICIDE

The first step in the analysis is the separation of friendly fire casualties from those that are the result of enemy weapons (henceforth, incidents of ship damage or loss are referred to as "casualties" or "ship casualties"). For this, a formal definition of fratricide is required. Since none exists (in a naval sense), one must be created.

> Fratricide: unintentionally causing injury to the personnel of one's own force, or damage to its equipment, as the result of an intent to engage a perceived enemy.

Simply stated, the incident must be a deliberate act thought to be directed against an enemy when, in fact, it was directed against one's own force. This definition, and thereby the study, keys on three crucial elements. First, the occurrence must be unintentional. This eliminates any occasion whereby friendly forces destroyed their own vessel in order to keep it from falling into the possession of an enemy. Second, an incident must be the result of an intention to engage an enemy, thus discriminating against accidents occurring either during training exercises or in the normal operation of a vessel. Finally, and perhaps most importantly, an enemy need not be present. It is sufficient that the attacker believes his target to be an enemy. This specification is essential to the study of naval fratricide, because naval combat need not always consist of great armadas of warships locked in an intense

9

duel. War at sea can consist of a lone submarine attacking
an unarmed merchant vessel or, more simply, a fishing
trawler laying mines. Fratricide is possible even in these
situations. Thus, for the purpose of this study, the
singular requirement for the existence of a "combat
situation" is the perception by any ship, submarine, or
aircraft of the threat of combat damage or the opportunity
to inflict it.

B.   CONTRAST WITH GROUND FRATRICIDE

Naval and ground friendly fire can be very different
in that vessels - not people - are the subjects. Despite
the importance of tanks and artillery, ground combat is
mostly thought of as being fought by soldiers. Fighting at
sea involves ships, submarines, and aircraft. Naval
systems are competing - not individual sailors. Whereas a
bomb, rocket, bullet, shell, and grenade can each with
great assurance kill or wound a man, it might take anywhere
from one to more than fifty direct hits to achieve the
significant wounding or destruction of a ship.

Because of this emphasis on systems, incidents of
friendly damage to vessels must be the basis of an analysis
of naval fratricide. Personnel casualty statistics are
important, but the measure of the combat power of a naval
force is its number of ships, submarines, and aircraft.
Therefore, this study concentrates on documented friendly
fire damage to United States ships and submarines in the
last major naval war: World War II. Incidents of naval air
force and merchant vessel fratricide, however significant,

are not included because of a present lack of complete and reliable data.

C. TYPES OF NAVAL FRATRICIDE

1. Surface, Submarine, and Aircraft Attack

Incidents of naval friendly fire can be separated into six types based on that which is a threat to a ship or submarine; the most obvious of these are surface (ships), submarine, and aircraft types. Less apparent are three instances of fratricide which, at first evaluation, do not appear to merit inclusion in the study but must be considered based on the guiding definition. These are incidents of damage or loss due to friendly mining, own-weapon failure, and collision.

2. Mining

A mine, like a ship or submarine, can be considered a unit of one's force; it is most like a missile that attacks the first target it detects. A mine has no ability to distinguish friend from foe; it considers every vessel an enemy. Passing through a friendly minefield (the most common cause of mine fratricide) is considered a combat situation since the threat of weapon damage exists. In fact, crews prepare for the traversing of friendly mined areas exactly as they would for battle; they bring their ships to their highest condition of damage control readiness.

3. Weapon Failure

The question of when to consider a weapon failure an incident of fratricide can be difficult. The general discriminating condition is whether or not the weapon was launched. Premature gunpowder detonation, racked depth charge explosions, and similar events are not considered friendly fire because the respective weapon was never sent in the direction of a target. Whether or not they take place during combat, such occurrences are dangers inherent in the normal operation of naval weapon systems. Aircraft crashes aboard aircraft carriers are similarly not included in the study regardless of the situation. The best examples of fratricidal weapon failures are circular-running torpedoes, acoustic-homing torpedoes that attack friendly ships or submarines, and launched depth charges that incidentally damage friendly vessels.

4. Collision

A collision is treated as an instance of friendly fire if it occurs in a combat situation. Since a naval engagement demands the maneuvering of the opposing forces, it follows that ship damage incurred during the battle through friendly collision should be considered combat-related. Ship collisions can cause substantial damage; their effect can be similar to that of any other naval weapon.

III. ANALYSIS

A. DATA SELECTION

1. Sources

The primary source for this study is the former Naval History Division's *United States Naval Chronology, World War II*.[1] This invaluable reference contains every incident of loss, sinking, and damage to U.S. naval forces (excluding naval air forces) occurring from the start of hostilities on 7 December 1941 until the signing of the surrender in Tokyo Bay.[2] Entries include the date, ship, hull number, cause of damage (horizontal bomber, submarine torpedo, naval gunfire, etc.), and the location of the subject vessel when it was damaged. Short narratives of strategic operations and noteworthy world events are also included.

Incidents of friendly fire are recorded as in the following example from the February 1945 section:

> 20, Tues.   Army troops under cover of Marine aircraft are landed on Biri Island, P. I., to insure control of San Bernardino Strait. (See 19 February 1945.)
> United States naval vessels damaged, Iwo Jima area:
> Light cruiser *Biloxi* (CL-80), accidentally by United States naval gunfire, 25°47'N., 141°15'E.
> Hospital ship *Samaritan* (AH-10), accidentally by United States naval gunfire, 24°46'N., 141°19'E.
> Attack transports *Napa* (APA-157) and *Logan* (APA-196), by collision, 24°46'N., 141°19'E.

---

[1] *Naval Chronology* was published in 1955. A revision updating the original with information resulting from additional research is due for publication in November 1999.

[2] The criteria by which an incident of damage is judged for entry into the *Chronology* is not specified. It is assumed that any damage requiring a significant repair effort (either underway by ship's company or in port) is included in this source.

         Attack cargo ship *Starr* (AKA-67), by collision,
         24°46'N.,
           141°19'E.
         LST-779, by coastal mortar, 24°46'N., 141°19'E.
       Japanese naval vessel sunk:
         Destroyer *Nokaze*, by submarine *Pargo* (SS-264), South
           China Sea, 12°48'N., 109°38'E.

The friendly fire data extracted from these entries appear
in chronological order in Appendices A through E. Appendix
A is the list of incidents of fratricide (or, in the case
of collisions, potential fratricide) involving all ships
and submarines. Appendices B through E are lists derived
from Appendix A and separated into the following ship
types: large (generally over 5000 tons displacement), small
(other than large), amphibious, and submarines. In each of
the spreadsheets, a loss is marked with an "X" and an
incident of damage is marked with a "Y."[3]

     The excerpt in the previous paragraph illustrates how
easily one can retrieve surface fratricide incidents from
the *Chronology*. Submarine, aircraft, and mine types are
similarly well marked. The difficulty, and consequently
what demanded the most research effort, was in the
identification of own weapon and combat collision
occurrences from the ambiguous entries in *Naval Chronology*.
Collisions are only listed as having taken place; in most
cases, no amplifying data such as the circumstances
surrounding the mishap appear. Occasionally, the "sunk" or
"damaged" list in an entry indicates the subject ships were
involved in a specific combat operation. As such, any

---

[3] In the collision column of Appendices A through E, some entries contain a "C" or an "N"
in addition to the loss or damage letter code ("X" or "Y"). This will be explained
later.

documented collision in the list was considered as having occurred during a combat situation. For example, the list of damaged vessels for the 10 July 1943 entry is titled "United States naval vessels damaged, Sicily landings: ". It indicates that two destroyers, an attack transport, two tank-landing ships (LST's), and a submarine chaser were involved in collisions. These incidents are deemed combat-related. Unfortunately, this type (specifying combat) is rare. Most, like "Iwo Jima area" in the sample excerpt, are geographic and thus ambiguous.

The *Dictionary of American Naval Fighting Ships Online* website was the best source for exploring the circumstances surrounding specific collisions. This reference would comprise several volumes in book form, and it contains biographical information on all commissioned vessels or other craft used by the Navy at any time in its history. The *Dictionary* is not perfect; entries that document collisions or friendly fire damage are scarce, and the website has not to date completed the transcription of many amphibious, auxiliary, and small craft from the book version. Despite this, valuable information was obtained. Additional sources were used to further investigate both collision data and possible instances of own weapon damage. These were Kemp's *Friend or Foe*, Theodore Roscoe's outstanding *United States Destroyer Operations in World War II*, and James Grace's *Naval Battle of Guadalcanal: Night Action, 13 November 1942*. In all, 44 of 169 collision incidents were identified as having or not having occurred during combat, and several possible occurrences of own weapon damage were excluded.

2. Collision Incident Sampling and Confidence Interval

An accurate separation of the collision data is crucial to this study because collisions dominate the total number of friendly fire incidents. From the data summation, there are 169 collisions documented in *Naval Chronology*; ten resulted in the loss of the vessel (X) and 158 caused significant damage (Y). Twenty of the 169 have been confirmed as not having occurred in combat. If the remaining 149 were combat-related, they would make up nearly 70 percent of the total number of fratricide cases for the war. Unfortunately, it was not possible to fully investigate every collision. The National Archives and Research Administration in College Park, Maryland, holds such documents as ship's logs and war diaries that could be used to further separate combat from non-combat collisions. The amount of research required for certainty, however, is too great given the time constraints of this thesis. Although less accurate than an exhaustive investigation, statistical sampling methods can provide a reasonable estimate of the total number of combat collisions based on the ratio of known combat to known non-combat incidents.

As previously stated, 44 collisions were positively identified as either combat or non-combat related; each is given an additional code letter "C" for being combat-related or "N" for being non-combat related. These specific incidents are referred to as *samples* of the total *population* of 169 collisions and are summarized from Appendix A as follows:

```
Sinking
        Non-combat (XN)    :  5
        Combat (XC)        :  0

Damage
        Non-combat (YN)    : 15
        Combat (YC)        : 24
```

Because none of the five sampled sinkings were combat-related, it is assumed that none of the ten collision sinkings in the total population were such. Hence, the number of ships sunk by any type of fratricide does not include a single incident of collision. Of the 39 sampled instances of collision damage, 62 percent were the result of combat operations; this proportion is known as an *estimator* because it is a best guess based on incomplete population data. Applying this proportion to the 157 total incidents of collision damage, 97 ships are estimated to have suffered significant damage in combat-related collisions. These calculations can be seen in Appendix F. Adding 97 to the number of friendly fire incidents of damage and loss of the remaining types in Appendix A results in an estimate of 162 total friendly fire incidents during the war.

The 62-percent estimator is, of course, not exact. The true value of the proportion of combat-related incidents of damage for the population can only be determined if all 169 incidents are separable. For this reason, we can only estimate the true proportion. The "margin of error" of the estimator can be computed, however, based on the number of samples, the size of the population, and the assumption that the estimator has an approximately normal distribution. Jay Devore, in *Probability and Statistics for Engineering and the Sciences*, explains:

> ...if the estimator has at least approximately a normal distribution, we can be quite confident that the true value lies within 2 or 3 standard deviations of the estimated value. (Devore, 1995, p. 275)

This error margin is called a *confidence interval* and is computed by adding and subtracting standard deviations of the estimator from its value.[4] Additionally, because the collision population is not infinite, the *finite population correction* can be applied that further reduces the size of the interval. (Cochran, 1977, p. 61) The completed calculations are shown in Appendix F; the result is an interval of (0.50, 0.73). This range is said to contain the true value of the combat damage proportion of the 169-collision population with 90 percent confidence.

B. STATISTICAL ANALYSIS AND INTERPRETATION

1. Proportions

The total incidents of fratricide loss and damage (using the estimate of 97 combat-related collisions) were

---

[4] See Devore, Chapter 7, for details.

compared to the war totals for loss and damage: 226 and 993 respectively.[5] These results are also shown in Appendix F. They are consistent with Hawkins' research into ground force fratricide in World War II in that the proportions are much higher than what might be expected. (Hawkins, 1994, p. 57) Six percent of the ships sunk and fifteen percent of the incidents of damage were the result of friendly fire. When combined, friendly forces caused thirteen percent of all cases of U.S. ship and submarine loss or damage in the war.

The minimum and maximum friendly fire totals and proportions were generated from the lower and upper bounds of the combat-related collision estimator confidence interval (0.50, 0.73), respectively. Just as the 62-percent estimator was used to estimate 97 combat-related collisions and 162 total friendly fire incidents, the interval's lower and upper bounds allow us to estimate a minimum and maximum number of combat collisions and corresponding friendly fire totals. The resulting lowest and highest probable number of total friendly fire incidents then yield the minimum and maximum friendly fire proportions seen in Appendix F. Thus, the percentage of fratricide casualties during World War II could have been twelve percent at a minimum and as high as fifteen percent.

---

[5] Total damage figure was obtained by counting incidents in *Naval Chronology*. Total losses figure was obtained by counting 174 losses in David Brown's *Warship Losses of World War Two* (Annapolis: Naval Institute Press), pp. 26-157, and adding 52 lost submarines from *U.S. Submarine Losses, World War II* (Washington: U.S. GPO, 1949), p. 15.

The dominant fratricide types of the full list of ships (in Appendix A) and the large, small, and amphibious sub-groups were identified and their proportions calculated. The results, shown at the bottom of Appendices A through D, are summarized in Table 1.

Table 1. Proportions of Friendly Fire Incidents by Ship Type

		surface	sub	air	own wpn	mine	collision
All ships	sunk	0.02	0.01	0.03	0.01	0.01	
	damaged	0.30		0.02			0.60
Large ships	sunk						
	damaged	0.38				0.02	0.60
Small ships	sunk	0.02	0.01	0.04	0.01		
	damaged	0.27		0.01			0.65
Amphibs	sunk						
	damaged	0.26					0.74

We can see that collisions are by far the most common type of friendly fire; they constitute nearly three-quarters of all amphibious ship fratricide incidents (tank-landing ships alone accounted for nearly twenty percent of all collisions) and roughly two-thirds of those involving both small and large ships. Naval gunfire is the second-greatest contributor to friendly fire. Damage and loss from friendly surface engagements make up more than one-third of the total for large ships and more than one-quarter for both small and amphibious ships.

A compelling result was obtained by examining the proportions of friendly fire mishaps that occurred in the last ten full months of the war; the data is displayed in Appendices A through D and summarized in Table 2.   This

Table 2.   Proportions of Surface and Collision Friendly Fire Incidents Occurring from October 1944 to August 1945 by Ship Type

	surface	collision
All ships	0.77	0.71
Large ships	0.94	0.78
Small ships	0.69	0.68
Amphibs	0.91	0.88

period was chosen to illustrate how the increase in fratricide cases could be linked to the increased number and intensity of combat operations through the last year of the war in the Pacific.   From October 1944 until August 1945, such events as the invasion of the Philippines, the Battle for Leyte Gulf, the first and subsequent use of the kamikaze, the capture of Iwo Jima, and the bloody three-month struggle for Okinawa dramatically increased the engagement rate and ferocity of the war to their greatest levels.   During these final months, surface forces endured the majority of their incidents of both friendly naval gunfire and collision.   Large and amphibious ships especially suffered in this time; over ninety percent of naval gunfire fratricide occurred for both ship types.

An essential part of this study is a numerical investigation into the occurrence of fratricide as a result of the intensity of specific types of combat operations. As the frequency and intensity of combat increase, then the number of battle casualties will naturally increase. If the occurrence of friendly fire is related to the total number of battle casualties, it follows that friendly fire is a function primarily of the frequency and intensity of combat. Thus, we must determine whether or not friendly fire casualties are dependent on the total number of casualties of any kind suffered by U.S. naval forces.

2. Linear Regression

Regression analysis can be used to determine the strength of the relationship between the total number of ship casualties and the number of fratricide ship casualties experienced by American naval forces in the war.[6] Figure 1 is a plot of the monthly damage and loss total (clear) and the corresponding monthly friendly fire total (shaded) for the war. Major operations and events are annotated to give a perspective of the time of occurrence of important and costly operations and battles. From an initial observation, the friendly fire count roughly follows the trend of the overall monthly casualties.

A regression was conducted using monthly total casualties as the independent variable and monthly friendly fire casualties as the dependent variable. The results are

---

[6] For details regarding the following discussion of regression analysis, see Lawrence Hamilton's *Regression with Graphics* (Belmont, CA: Wadsworth, 1992), Chapter 2.

Figure 1. American Ship Casualties by month

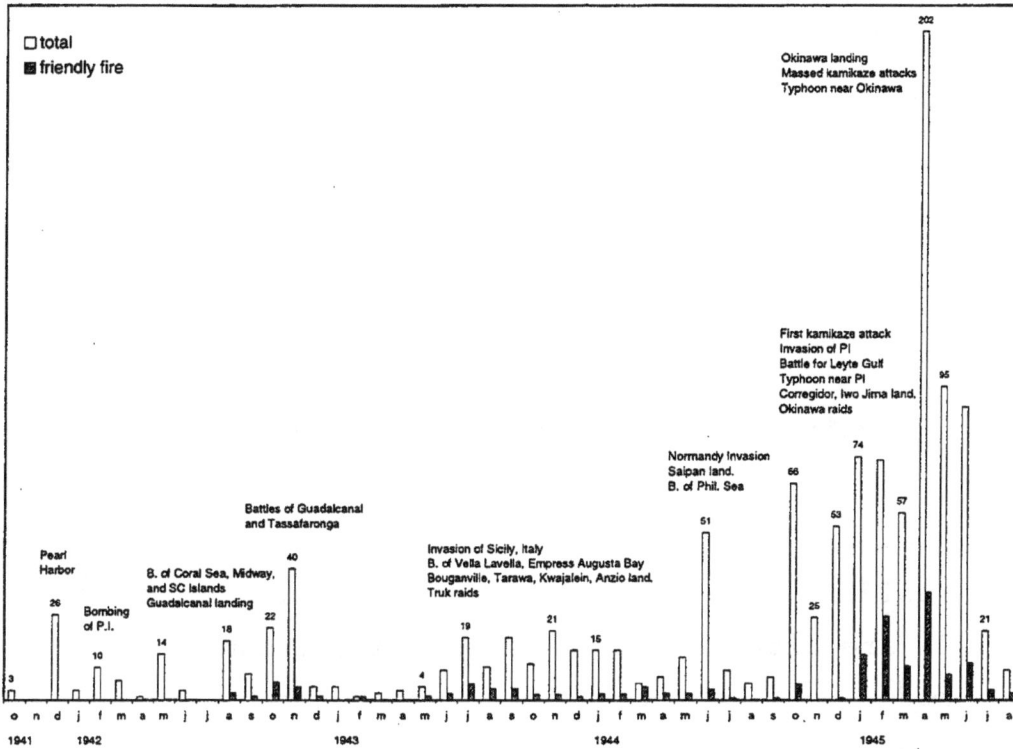

shown as the linear fit in Figure 2a and the residual plot
in Figure 2b. The former is a graph of each actual
friendly fire observation (Y) and its corresponding linear
estimate (Predicted Y). On this plot we can see how the
real data compare to the regressed estimates for each value
of the monthly total casualty data set. The vertical
distance between each pair is known as a *residual*; these
distances indicate how far each predicted value is from its
matching real value. A relatively high residual value
indicates that the real data point on which it is based
does not fit well into the linear regression of the data
set. From the residual plot we can see which estimated
values have the highest and lowest residual values.

23

Figure 2a. Linear Regression of Friendly Fire Totals

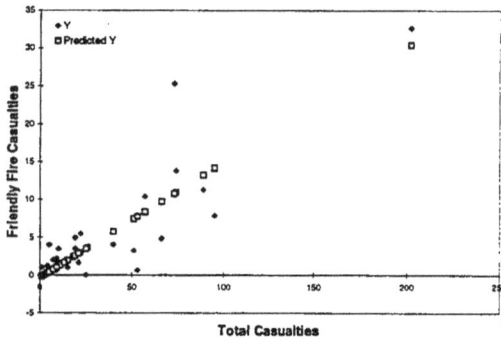

Figure 2b. Residual Plot

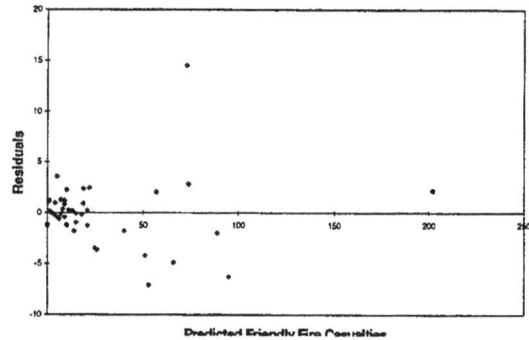

Graphical Results of Regression of Monthly Friendly Fire
and Total Casualties

A residual plot also gives an indication of how the
residuals are distributed. An essential assumption of the
linear model is that the residuals should be distributed
normally with the same mean and variance and be unrelated
to the total casualty variable and each other. The
residual plot is an easy way to check, among other things,
for normally distributed residuals.

The linear fit of this regression is adversely
influenced by there having been no fratricide casualties
during the first ten months of the war (as seen in Figure 1
and Appendix G). This has the effect of masking the
relationship between the number of casualties of all types
and the number of those resulting from fratricide during
the remainder of the war. Not considering data from this
period improves the fit of the regression. This may seem
to be a manipulation of data to "get a good fit," but it

24

can be justified, since the qualitative and quantitative nature of combat was different during these two periods.

The first months of the war accounted for 66 incidents of damage and loss; this is only five percent of the American ship and submarine casualties of the entire war. The major events in this period were the Pearl Harbor attack and the Battles of the Coral Sea and Midway. Pearl Harbor was a completely one-sided aircraft attack. Coral Sea and Midway were, again, dominated by air power; because the fleets never came into sight of one another, there were no surface engagements and no real chance of friendly fire being inflicted on these vessels. Potential fratricide lay in the attack of surface vessels by aircraft of their own force, but this simply did not occur. The forces were too far separated to be mistaken for one another by a pilot in the heat of battle. Although undisciplined anti-aircraft gunnery could have caused some friendly fire incidents, no cases were documented.

The point where an approximate linear relationship between fratricide and combat casualties becomes apparent is after the first offensive amphibious landings were made in the Pacific. In August 1942, the following islands in the Solomon group were invaded (among others): Tulagi, Gavutu, and, most importantly, Guadalcanal. From then on, the patterns of fluctuation of the numbers of total and fratricide casualties are strikingly similar. The Normandy invasion and the great surface battles of the Pacific had not yet been fought. Additionally, kamikaze attacks were

25

still two years away. Hence, with regard to the frequency
and intensity of naval combat, the first ten months of 1942
were atypical of the rest of the war and will be de-
emphasized in subsequent regression analyses.

Another problem in the first regression can be seen
from the residual plot in Figure 2b. The linear fit is
good for months in which the total ship casualties are less
than 25; the value of each residual is small. These values
start to increase, however, for months with greater than 25
casualties. This indicates that the variation in
fratricide increases with increasing total casualties and
is not consistent with basic linear regression assumptions.
If the assumptions were valid, the residual plot would have
its points fairly evenly scattered over the range of values
of the friendly fire estimates (called a "clear" plot).

The problem with regressing data with varying
variances is that the data points with the larger residuals
have a larger effect on the slope and y-intercept of the
regression line. So, in Figure 2a, the data points in the
lower left-hand corner have an effect on the regression
line that is too small. One solution to this difficulty is
a power transformation of the data. Successive roots of
both the monthly casualty and fratricide totals were taken
and regressions performed.

The final model is plotted in Figures 3a and 3b.
These show a regression of the square roots of the friendly
fire data with the cube roots of the total casualty data

Figure 3a. Linear Regression of Friendly Fire Totals

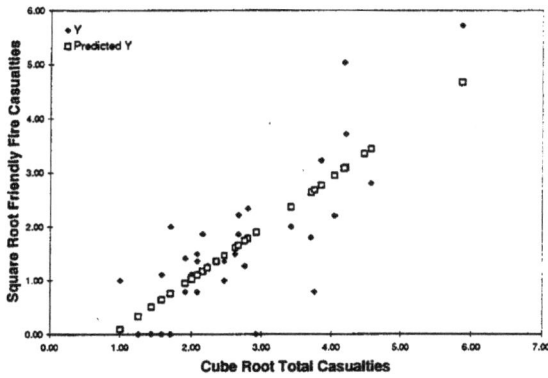

Figure 3b. Residual Plot

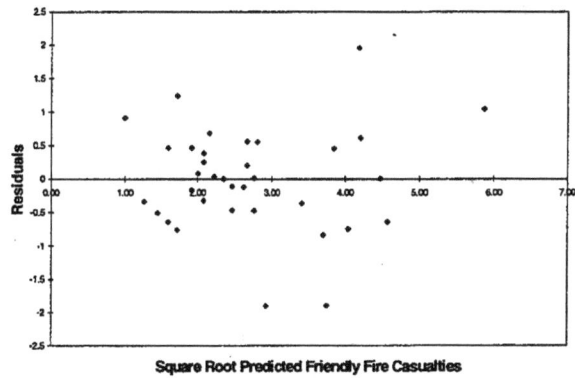

Graphical Results of Regression of Square Root Monthly Friendly Fire
and Cube Root Monthly Total Casualties

(excluding the first ten months). This regression was
initially selected because its residual plot was the most
clear (meaning its residuals were the most normally
distributed). The resulting model is

$$(incidents\ of\ fratricide)^{1/2} = 0.9396 * (total\ casualties)^{1/3} - 0.8489$$

Rewriting this with a first order dependent variable gives

$$incidents\ of\ fratricide = [0.9396 * (total\ casualties)^{1/3} - 0.8489]^2$$

This model gives the estimated proportion of
fratricide incidents over the course of the war as 12.4
percent. This value is near the 13.3 percent obtained from
the raw data, and it is the closest of all the transformed-
data regressions performed. Its R^2 and R_a^2 statistics,
measures of the strength of the linear relationship between
the dependent and independent variables, are 0.645 and

0.634 respectively. With 1 being a perfect positive linear relationship, the values of these statistics indicate a relatively strong connection between the monthly casualty total and the monthly fratricide casualty total. Though not accurate for each month, the model is reliable over the course of the war.

Several regressions with varying data transformations were carried out on the data from the entire war (not excluding any months) and the resulting proportions calculated. The results of all regressions are shown in Appendix H. The monthly estimates of friendly fire incidents (based on the total number of casualties in each month) and the corresponding fratricide proportion of each model are displayed in columns. The first two models use the non-transformed data. Square-root, cube-root, and fourth-root transformations of both dependent and independent variables are labeled as follows: sqrt, 3rt, and 4rt. "Mix" indicates the square-root friendly fire and cube-root total casualty regressions. "Cut" indicates a model that excludes the first ten months of data.

These statistical models are less accurate in estimating the true friendly fire proportion than their cut-data counterparts (with the first ten months excluded). The square-root friendly fire and cube-root total casualty model of the full data set yields a friendly fire percentage of only 10.8. Other regressions similarly fell short of the 13.3 percent estimated from the raw data. Again, the purpose of the regression analysis in this study is not to model the monthly occurrence of friendly fire but to establish a dependence of fratricide on the occurrence of battle casualties. Despite any inaccuracies in estimating the raw data fratricide percentage, all of the valid linear models strongly suggest that such a dependence exists.

3. Poisson Process Applicability

An interesting possibility regarding the incidence of friendly fire was realized after further examination of the residual plot in Figure 2b. The information therein suggests that fratricide casualties could occur according to a *Poisson* distribution.[7]

In Figure 2b we see that, as the numbers of estimated friendly fire casualties increase, the variability in the corresponding residuals increases. As such, the variance of the actual friendly fire data increases as the friendly fire incident rates increase. If the number of incidents of fratricide in a given month is distributed as a Poisson random variable with parameter λ (casualties per month), the expected value and variance of the number of fratricide incidents occurring each month would both be λ. An increase or decrease in the estimated rate of friendly fire would result in a corresponding increase or decrease in the estimated number and variance of such incidents. Thus, we would expect to see a result similar to Figure 2b: the

---

[7] For details of the following discussion, see Devore, Chapter 3, and Ross, Chapter 5.

variance of the actual friendly fire casualties increases with higher values of the friendly fire estimates.

In a Poisson-modeled battle, incidents of damage and loss to friendly and enemy forces, also known as blue and red forces respectively, occur at certain rates. These are denoted as λ_{blue} and λ_{red}. If the rates of damage of blue and red forces are proportional to each other, then we have

$$\lambda_{red} = k_1 \lambda_{blue} \tag{1}$$

where k_1 is a proportionality constant reflecting the relative skills of red and blue. If blue weapons cause damage to both red and blue forces, then resulting rates of blue self-damage (fratricide) should be proportional to the observed damage inflicted on red. Therefore, the rate of blue fratricide, λ_{frat}, is

$$\lambda_{frat} = k_2 \lambda_{red} \tag{2}$$

where k_2 is a proportionality constant governed by tactical doctrine, identification procedures, and all other means to keep blue fire that is damaging red from also damaging blue. By combining equations (1) and (2), we can express the rate of blue friendly fire as such:

$$\lambda_{frat} = k_1 k_2 \lambda_{blue} \tag{3}$$

Initially, we sought a dependence of fratricide casualties on the total number of casualties for each month of the war using regression analysis. Equation (3) illustrates that,

30

for the Poisson model, a dependence is valid, but the relationship will be better understood by knowledge of three parameters: k_1 and k_2, which for some not too lengthy time can be treated as constants, and λ_{blue}, which is the varying intensity of blue's combat activities.

Unfortunately, the time constraints of this thesis were such that an in-depth Poisson analysis was not possible. Hence, Poisson process modeling of fratricide remains an excellent topic for future research.

4. Submarines

Submarines deserve special attention in this study because they generally did not operate with surface forces. As such, they were exposed to dissimilar combat situations. While aircraft carriers and battleships vigorously sought out and engaged their opposites, submarines were (and still are) at their optimal combat effectiveness when completely hidden from the enemy. In most cases, they independently patrolled either an assigned sector or an important geographic area and preyed on targets of opportunity. For example, German *wolfpacks* were not groups of U-boats that hunted collectively. They were clusters of lone submarines drawn together for massed attacks on Allied merchant convoys. Additionally, submarine combat was unique in that it was rarely fought between submarines. Direct action with an adversary most often took the form of diving and evading a surface or air attack. In these cases, the submarine was most likely trying to elude the enemy rather than attempting to destroy him.

Cases of mistaken identity were relatively frequent, however, primarily because of the peculiar situation in which a submarine finds itself when approached by patrolling ships or aircraft. The act of submerging, a safe play by the captain regardless of the identity of the approaching ship or planes, was in many cases interpreted by captains and pilots as an "admission of guilt" of being an enemy; the submarine was depth-charged or bombed accordingly. It is no surprise, then, that aircraft attacks on friendly submarines numbered higher than any other type of fratricide incident in Kemp's study. (Kemp, 1995, p. 93) Attacks by surface vessels on submarines were often initiated solely by acoustic detection (despite the near impossibility of positive identification of the submarine). For example, the American submarine *Seawolf* was underway in the area of the U.S. Seventh Fleet on a mission to deliver supplies and personnel to the island of Samar in October 1943. After the torpedoing of one of Seventh Fleet's screening ships, the destroyer escort USS *Rowell* gained sonar contact on *Seawolf* thinking she was the attacker. The target was repeatedly hedgehogged, and a large air bubble and debris were observed floating to the surface.[8] *Seawolf* never returned from her mission, and a subsequent investigation revealed that *Rowell* had sent her to the bottom.

---

[8] The *hedgehog* was a weapon system that quickly fired multiple underwater explosives such that the resulting pattern covered a greater area than that of conventional depth charges.

The fratricide percentage of the U.S. submarine force
was calculated based only on losses (the small number of
documented incidents of submarine damage does not provide
for useful analysis). The results are displayed in
Appendix E. The proportion is eight percent: four friendly
sinkings out of 52 losses. This is similar to the six-
percent figure for American surface combatants. What is
disturbing is that two of the four losses were the result
of weapon failures. The submarines *Tang* and *Tullibee* were
the victims of circular running torpedoes. These are
malfunctioning weapons that, upon release, swim in a near
circle and arrive after a short time at their firing point.
These "rogue" torpedoes were not uncommon; there are many
incidents of a firing submarine being forced to conduct
evasive maneuvers to avoid being struck by its own torpedo.
Surface vessels were not immune to such incidents. In
March 1942 the cruiser HMS *Trinidad* was damaged by her own
launched torpedo while protecting a convoy bound for
Russia. (Kemp, 1995, pp. 150-152) Fortunately for the
Americans, the *Tang* and *Tullibee* occurrences were the only
friendly fire weapon failures of any of their ship types
during the war.

For comparison, Appendix E also shows the fratricide
percentage of German submarines in World War II; of almost
eight hundred U-boats lost, only 12 - a mere one-and-a-half
percent - were sunk by friendly fire.[9] Several factors
could account for this low proportion, the most significant

being the relatively small part played by the surface
Kriegsmarine in the war and the general containment of the
Luftwaffe over continental Europe after the Battle of
Britain. German submarines traveled all over the Atlantic
and into the Indian and Pacific Oceans, and for the most
part they were never supported, much less encountered, by
German warships. Contact with the *Luftwaffe* was similarly
infrequent. For whatever reason, the Germans' low friendly
fire rate is impressive given the intensity of the U-boat
campaign in the Battle of the Atlantic.

A better comparison between American and German
submarine fratricide losses can be made with the German
statistics of World War I (shown in Appendix E). Of 178 U-
boats lost, fifteen (eight percent) were the result of
friendly fire. This is nearly identical to the American
submarine fratricide proportion in World War II.
Interestingly, like the U.S. losses in the 1940's, half of
the World War I German losses were caused by weapon
failures; all but one failure involved the destruction of
mine-laying submarines by their own laid mines.

---

[9] Fratricide totals for both World War I and II were obtained by counting incidents in
Paul Kemp's *U-boats Destroyed* (Annapolis: Naval Institute Press, 1997). Total loss
figures are from the same book, page 7.

IV.   THE NATURE OF NAVAL FRATRICIDE

A.   CAUSES

Incidents of fratricide have both causes and contributing factors. A cause is that which directly results in friendly fire such as misidentifying a target. A contributing factor helps to create a situation in which fratricide is possible. For instance, inadequate identification procedures or a lack of recognition training may contribute to misidentification. It should be noted that, given the number of vessels and aircraft involved in combat operations in all theaters of the war, the measures taken to protect friendly forces from one another were extremely effective. However, as the following discussion illustrates, the slightest human error or oversight was enough to cause significant damage and loss of life.

1.   Misidentification

The single greatest cause of naval fratricide is mistaking a friend for an enemy. Ship silhouettes in any condition of visibility are difficult to positively identify. At the time of the Second World War, several warship classes of one country had very similarly shaped counterparts in other navies. The angle of observation often confounds a ship's identity, as looking down the length of a vessel, especially from stern to bow, provides almost no distinguishing information when compared to a ship's beam aspect. Haze, fog, and other atmospheric conditions obscure details and can reduce the image of any ship into a shapeless gray mass. In many cases, especially at night, identification is only possible when the range is closed to a mere few hundred yards.

World War II submarines were the most difficult to distinguish, primarily because the boats of many countries had very similar shapes. Since they lay low in the water, the only visible portion of a submarine was the conning tower. Thus, there was far less detail by which one could differentiate than when dealing with surface vessels. The aircraft of World War II were just as difficult to identify because the shapes of the majority them were fundamentally identical. In addition to a plane's small size and great speed, its altitude and atmospheric conditions such as cloud cover, haze, and sun glare dramatically reduce the likelihood of proper identification.

2. Psychological Effects

Friendly fire is also caused by the psychological effect of being constantly prepared for the sudden eruption of battle. This sort of expectation, a combination of fear and anxiety, in many cases has led to the misidentification of even the most distinctly friendly vessels. The British, having already survived one U-boat onslaught twenty years before, were extremely concerned over the German submarine menace of World War II. Convoy escort captains, anti-submarine aircraft pilots, and anyone on guard against U-boat activity were keenly aware of what each destroyed U-boat meant to the survival of their country. Unfortunately, this zealous attitude was as dangerous to

their own submarines as it was to the Germans', as is noted
by British submariner Lieutenant John Coote:

> All the restrictions in the world didn't
> guarantee immunity from a keyed-up Wellington
> [aircraft] pilot dropping out of the overcast
> and seeing his first ever U-boat right in front
> of him with Distinguished Service Order written
> all over it.[10]

Such a reaction is understandable from one who is
placed in a situation in which he may lose his life. The
instinctive response upon sighting any vessel in an area
that might contain an enemy is to assume that the vessel is
an enemy. The ever-present possibility of losing one's
ship can motivate even the most careful skipper to open
fire on a target before its identity is established.
Interestingly enough, a lack of such vigilance can be just
as deadly. The sinking of the German destroyer *Friedrich
Eckholdt* on New Year's Eve 1942 was the result of her
skipper misidentifying the British cruiser *Sheffield* for
one of his own. When the German ship approached, the
British gunners sank her in a matter of minutes. (Kemp,
1995, pp. 24-26)

The hunt for the German battleship *Bismarck* provides
an excellent example of how the expectation of contact with
the enemy can deceive one into attacking a friend. May
1941 witnessed one of the greatest pursuits in naval
history. On the 24th, *Bismarck* sank the battle cruiser

---

[10] Kemp, *Friend or Foe*, p. 94. The Distinguished Service Order is England's second-most
senior award for gallantry. Early in the war, it was given as a standard reward for
sinking a U-boat.

Hood, the pride of the Royal Navy, in a fight lasting only six minutes. Out of some 1400 crew, only three survived. Outraged and bent on vengeance, the HMS *Ark Royal* carrier group immediately gave chase. Early on the 26th, the cruiser *Sheffield* was detached by the group commander (aboard HMS *Renown*) with orders to close the German battleship and maintain contact on her. Later that day, as British ships from all over the area left their assignments to join the hunt, *Ark Royal* launched the first of two aircraft strikes against the German battleship. Unaware that *Sheffield* had steamed ahead between the two forces, her pilots had been briefed that the first ship they made contact with would be *Bismarck*. As a result, the British torpedo planes mistakenly attacked *Sheffield* despite the near impossibility of confusing her for the larger German ship.

> *Ark Royal*'s aircrew were thoroughly familiar with the *Sheffield*; the two ships had steamed thousands of miles together in company. Moreover *Bismarck* was five times the cruiser's tonnage, was nearly 300 feet longer and had one funnel as opposed to *Sheffield*'s two. It might seem impossible for the aircrew to fail to identify *Sheffield* but they only saw what they expected to see. (Kemp, 1995, p. 48)

The mental state of "excessive combat readiness" can also lead to identification procedures being completely ignored. On the day of the Japanese attack on Pearl Harbor, the submarine USS *Thresher* had returned to Hawaii from a 48-day patrol. To ensure submarines were able to approach friendly harbors without fear of attack from coastal defenses, surface escorts were detailed to

accompany each boat. Having prematurely detached her
escort before reaching the harbor, *Thresher* was ordered to
wait for another (a wise decision based on the day's
previous events). A destroyer appeared at the rendezvous;
unknown to *Thresher* it was not her new escort. As the
submarine surfaced, the destroyer assumed she was a
Japanese boat and immediately opened fire with her guns.
She dived and remained underwater until the next morning.
Upon surfacing she was again attacked, this time by an
airplane. Submerging once more, she was brought into port
later that day by a destroyer. It is not hard to
understand why the both the destroyer and aircraft crews
were so aggressive; America's worst military disaster was
only hours old, the entire naval district was on combat
alert, and Japanese submarines were known to have been in
the area. (Kemp, 1995, pp. 73-74)

Fear of the dreaded *kamikaze* resulted in numerous
occurrences of friendly fire in which identification was
not an issue. In March 1945, during the Okinawa campaign,
the U.S. aircraft carrier *Enterprise* was one of several
vessels significantly damaged by stray anti-aircraft
gunfire intended to destroy attacking Japanese suicide
planes. The terror created by these human weapons was so
great that gunners frequently forgot or ignored weapon
safety arcs and fired directly into neighboring ships. In
this case, *Enterprise* was so badly shot up that for a time
she was unable to either launch or recover aircraft.

B. CONTRIBUTING FACTORS

1. Identification Procedures and IFF

Again, a contributing factor is one that helps to create a situation in which friendly fire is possible. One of the most common of these is the failure of identification procedures. For surface vessels and surfaced submarines, identification was generally established using some form of a challenge-and-reply system whereby a ship would, with a signal lamp, send a coded challenge to another. The ship would then wait for the corresponding reply; if a proper response was not received, the initiator could consider the other an enemy. Problems arose, however, when directional lamps were used to issue challenges. If a ship did not see a poorly aimed challenge, the first she might know about it would be upon the arrival of shells from the signaling ship.

In March 1943 a Royal Navy motor launch was rammed and sunk by the British corvette *Burdock* because of an inadequate signal light. Noticing that the corvette had turned to ram, the commanding officer of the launch quickly issued the challenge with a shaded blue lamp. The corvette did not see the signal, and the launch was split in two in the ensuing collision. It is interesting to note that the two vessels were not made aware of each other's presence in the area by their mutual parent command, and the corvette men were still "keyed up" from a recent unsuccessful attack on a presumed enemy submarine. (Kemp, 1995, p. 36)

Other identification methods included colored signal
flares, grenades, or "fighting lights" rigged on a ship for
display in any number of shapes and color combinations.
Flares and grenades were used especially by submarines when
approached by aircraft (when speed was of the essence).
The following description illustrates the seriousness given
to these procedures by submariners:

> The cry of "Signalman on the Bridge" was the
> call for everyone else in the boat to get out
> of the way or flatten themselves against the
> bulkhead.   Speed   was   of   the   essence   in
> answering   or   giving   a   challenge   and   the
> signalman would not waste time on apologies if
> someone was flattened or sent flying in his
> rush to get to the bridge. (Kemp, 1995, p. 16)

The principal limitation of the challenge-and-reply
system was its dependence on good visibility.
Additionally, a vessel initiating a challenge could create
for itself a serious disadvantage. An enemy could easily
recognize a foreign challenge or lighting configuration and
immediately open fire on its originator. Also, ships
during mêlée and night actions often did not have time to
wait for positive identification before engaging potential
targets; any hesitation to open fire was a severe risk.
Consequently, an electronic system - Identification Friend
or Foe (IFF) - was developed in 1938 to assist forces in
such situations. A ship using radar was able to identify
allies by means of a special "blip" on its radar screen.
It was useful in that identification of several contacts
could be made quickly and without visually giving away
one's position. Despite such concerns as an enemy

electronically masking itself as a friend, the system became popular - so much so that it is in use in many of today's naval forces.

As with all measures to counter friendly fire, IFF had its limitations. Reliance on the system as the "cure" for misidentification led to an incident between American destroyers during the Battle of Empress Augusta Bay in November 1943. USS *Spence* had just engaged the Japanese destroyer *Hatsukaze* when she began taking fire from ships of Arleigh Burke's Destroyer Division 45. After several near-miss salvoes, officers aboard *Spence* identified their attackers as friendly destroyers, and the situation was quickly cleared up. As it was, *Spence*'s IFF set had not been working. Ultimately, though, the mistake took place because the captains of DesDiv 45 made no attempt to back up their IFF information visually.

2. Control and Coordination of Forces

The human errors that cause friendly fire are not restricted to those made at the scene; many incidents are the result of the mistakes of non-participants taking place days or weeks before. The poor control and coordination of forces is an extremely subtle and potentially significant factor in naval fratricide. "Force level" commands are defined as those having operational control of groups of ships or exercising authority over the operations or movement of forces in a specific geographic area. Harbor, squadron, and fleet commands (and their air force

equivalents) are the most common of these. As we have seen
in the *Sheffield-Bismarck* and *Burdock* incidents, the loss
of situational awareness of commanders, lack of
communication within the command, and generally sloppy
staff work at the force level can be deadly. Poor
communication between independent commands operating forces
in a common area has similarly resulted in friendly fire
incidents. In fact, this type of human failure directly
caused two of the worst cases of naval fratricide in
history.

The most terrible naval friendly fire disaster is
without a doubt that which involved the German destroyer
Leberecht Maass. In February 1940, she set out as part of
a raid on British fishing trawlers operating off the Dogger
Bank. *Maass* was at the end of a column of six destroyers
that included *Max Schultz* and *Theodore Riedel*. On the
night of the 22nd, the force was overflown by a German
aircraft while proceeding through a narrow swept channel in
a British minefield off Schillig Roads. Before becoming a
renowned U-boat ace, Peter Cremer was assigned to *Riedel*
and gives the following account:

> As gunnery officer I was stationed on the
> bridge. At 1930 we sighted what appeared to be
> an enemy plane... While we recognized the Heinkel
> III and its German markings in time to avoid a
> mistake, the aircraft went into attack and at
> 1944 struck the last ship, *Leberecht Maass*,
> between bridge and forward funnel with a 50-
> kilo bomb. The destroyer veered to the right,
> dropped out of line and lost course - a secret
> course intended to give us a passage clear of
> mines. (Cremer, 1984, p. 8)

The aircraft returned and hit *Maass* again between the funnels; she broke in two and sank rapidly. The squadron commander ordered all ships to lower boats for rescue, and he placed *Riedel* and *Schultz* in anti-submarine screening positions. Cremer continues:

> Minutes later…*Max Schultz* blew up with a roar. We all now assumed we were under attack from enemy submarines, particularly as in the listening room they claimed to be picking up typical underwater noises. When the lookout on the forward gun reported 'bubble tracks sighted'…four depth charges flew overboard [from *Riedel*] in a high arc and the explosions shook us. Electric fuses jumped out and…the electric steering gear was momentarily jammed. *Theodore Riedel* began to rotate like a circus horse… (Cremer, 1984, p. 8)

Riedel's own-weapon fratricide with her depth charges is almost laughable compared to the damage inflicted on the force as a whole. Two destroyers were lost; 270 men from *Maass* and all 308 from *Schultz* - which no doubt struck a mine - were either killed outright or drowned in the freezing water. (Cremer, 1984, p. 9)

Adolf Hitler ordered an immediate inquiry into the incident. It revealed that *Fliegerkorps X*, responsible for the German bomber, had informed the destroyer group's parent command *Gruppe West* that its airplanes would be conducting anti-shipping operations in the area in question. *Gruppe West* sent its destroyers into the same area without informing *Fliegerkorps X* until after a flight of Heinkel 111 torpedo bombers had taken off on their patrol. *Gruppe West*'s commander attempted an excuse of the tragedy in the following manner:

> The destroyers knew that the appearance of friendly aircraft was constantly to be reckoned with. A continuous briefing could never make matters clearer since various air force units appeared in the area without the knowledge of the *Gruppe*. (Kemp, 1995, p. 45)

Thus, two destroyers and almost 600 men had been lost because of the appalling lack of communication between *Luftwaffe* and *Kriegsmarine* commands exercising control of forces in a common area.

A similar catastrophe struck the Royal Navy in August 1944 in the wake of the Normandy invasion. Four minesweepers of the British 1st Minesweeping Flotilla (MSF) had been clearing mines off Le Havre in preparation for a shore bombardment by a British battleship force and a subsequent landing by Canadian troops. Before the field was completely cleared, the 1st MSF received a new assignment to begin sweeping the Portsmouth/Arromanche area. On the 25th of the month, the navigator of HMS *Jason* (the senior ship) was sent to MSF headquarters aboard HMS *Ambitious* to insist upon the full clearance of the Le Havre minefield before starting work at Arromanche. His account is as follows:

> We knew full well that the clearance and search of the area off Le Havre had not been completed…[the] clearance was urgently needed to permit a heavy force to use the area to bombard the Le Havre coastal region…I was not received [aboard *Ambitious*] with any particular enthusiasm as all the staff officers were at supper. However, I made my point and was promised that the orders would be amended to

allow the 1st MSF to complete its unfinished
search and clearance. (Kemp, 1995, p. 55)

The modified orders were received in *Jason* two days later,
and the four-ship force set out. The weather was sunny
with good visibility, and just before midday the group was
flown over by a RAF aircraft bearing its distinguishable
black and white D-day stripes. Not much thought was given
to the plane until an hour-and-a-half later when a flight
of RAF Typhoons dove out of the sun and, with rockets and
machine gun fire, pounded the sweeper *Britomart* into a
floating wreck in a matter of minutes. Another, HMS
Hussar, was similarly battered and sank soon after. A
third ship, *Salamander*, had her stern blown off by a direct
rocket hit to her racks of depth charges. *Jason* and two
accompanying tugs were severely damaged by repeated
strafing.

The inevitable inquiry into this debacle uncovered the
distinguishable pattern of staff error common to many
fratricide incidents. The day that the sweepers set out
for Le Havre, they were detected by a British shore radar
installation; the operators had not been notified of any
friendly ships in the area on that day, so the group was
classified as hostile and Flag Officer British Assault Area
(FOBAA) sent a plane to confirm their identity. The ships
were located and identified by the aircrew as possibly
friendly. As such, FOBAA attempted to contact the MSF
headquarters staff aboard HMS *Ambitious* to make certain
that no friendly minesweepers were in the area.
Unfortunately for the 1st MSF, the telephone broke down and

FOBAA did not pursue the issue of identification. Instead, they sent a flight of eight rocket-armed Typhoons to destroy the ships. Upon arrival at the scene the flight leader identified the sweepers as probably friendly. He questioned the attack order twice, but FOBAA finally pushed him to engage. (Kemp, 1995, pp. 54-64)

An inquiry concluded "Staff work fell short of the highest standards in several respects." (Kemp, 1995, p. 63) In addition to the failure of the MSF staff officers to properly inform the numerous other service commands in the area of the sweeping schedule for that day, FOBAA astonishingly insisted on an attack against ships identified on several occasions as "probably friendly." These inexcusable errors cost the Royal Navy 78 men killed, 149 wounded, and three minesweepers lost.

A final example of staff negligence describes the only friendly fire attack made by an American submarine during the war. On 23 January 1945, the submarine *Guardfish* was near Guam returning from patrol when it made visual contact with another vessel. *Guardfish* was in a Joint Zone; this was an area in which ships and submarines were allowed to operate but were required to have positive identification of another vessel before attacking. The submarine's skipper sent a contact report to both Commander Submarines Pacific (Pearl Harbor) and Commander Task Group 17.7 (Guam) requesting information on friendly ships that might be in the area. *Guardfish* was subsequently ordered to maintain contact on her target, and, soon after, word was received from Guam that there were no friendly ships in her area. Both the commanding and executive officer identified the unknown vessel as a Japanese I-class submarine and the Americans positioned themselves for an attack. Four torpedoes were fired and two hits sent the target to the bottom; only when *Guardfish* began picking up the survivors was it realized that the mysterious target was the salvage ship USS *Extractor*.

The official inquiry into the disaster concluded that CTG 17.7 was unaware of *Extractor*'s presence in the area. The staff had ordered her to return to port, but receipt of the signal was never confirmed. For whatever reason, it was assumed that *Extractor* had received the order and was returning to the harbor. Based on this supposition, *Guardfish* was informed that no friendly ships were near her prior to the attack. It matters not that this event was small compared to the previous examples; staff carelessness and indolence unnecessarily cost six men their lives. (Kemp, 1995, pp. 147-149)

3. Force Separation Doctrine

As alluded to in the previous example, force separation doctrine is a key factor in preventing a ship or submarine from being in an area where an ally is expecting to find an enemy. The most common form of separation in the Second World War was for the protection of submarines; boats on patrol were usually assigned exclusive patrol sectors. If each stayed within its area, the likelihood of a submarine attacking a friend was minimal. Submarines were also protected from friendly surface and air attack by means of what the Royal Navy called a Moving Haven. This was a safety zone around the boat's estimated position in which friendly forces were not allowed to attack submarines. Near ports, Total Bombing Restriction areas and Submarine Sanctuaries attempted to ensure the safe passage of a submarine into and out of harbors and coastal regions.

Force separation existed in many forms. Aircraft returning from strikes or patrols were given specific directions from which they were allowed to approach their carriers safely. Ships used secret channels (known as "Q routes") which guaranteed safe passage through their own minefields. Breakdowns usually occurred as a result of the inaccuracy of navigation - especially aircraft navigation over the open sea - in the 1940's. Submarines would occasionally stray into a neighboring sector, or they were attacked in sanctuaries by friendly aircraft as a result of the aircrew's calculated position being in error sometimes by dozens of miles. Two U.S. ships - the destroyer *Tucker* and the converted luxury liner *President Coolidge* - were the victims of force separation failure; they both were mined and sunk in the same field off the island of Espiritu Santo. Still, these were the only two incidents of their type, and the small numbers of American submarines lost to surface and air forces (only two) indicate that submarine separation measures worked extremely well.

V. CONCLUSIONS AND RECOMMENDATIONS

A. CONCLUSIONS

The proportion of U.S. ships and submarines damaged or lost as a result of fratricide in World War II is thirteen percent; if the U.S. Navy is involved in a future conflict against a first-rate naval force, friendly fire will play a similarly significant role. Despite advances in weapon, IFF, navigation, and combat systems technologies, fratricide will exist wherever the potential for human error - at any level - exists. The factors that increase this potential will also increase the likelihood of incurring friendly fire casualties.

The most modern ground forces in the history of warfare fought for the liberation of Kuwait in 1991, and the resulting friendly fire percentage was seventeen percent. Almost thirty years before, Hawkins experienced similar rates as an infantry commander in Vietnam. (Hawkins, 1994, p. 57) As previously discussed, his article cites surveys of specific World War II operations in which fratricide proportions ranged from ten to fourteen percent. Hence, despite new technology (some of which is specifically designed to "clear up" confusion on the battlefield), ground combat fratricide levels have remained constant or have grown over the greater part of this century. Therefore, we can expect naval friendly fire percentages in future conflicts similar to that of World War II.

The number of naval fratricide casualties (like that of ground forces) is directly related to the frequency and intensity of naval combat. The regression analysis conducted in this study supports this conclusion. As such, there is no "learning curve"; neither the length of time of a conflict nor the battle experience of its combatants has a significant effect on the occurrence of friendly fire.

B. RECOMMENDATIONS

The U.S. Navy must acknowledge the substantial role fratricide has played in its history. The rate of friendly fire in future naval conflicts will not substantially decrease until the problem is taken seriously. When this happens, technology and operational doctrine can be developed such that they will equally serve both the need to destroy the enemy and the desire to protect our own forces from friendly weapons.

The Navy should also realize that its greatest weakness is not having been challenged in combat since 1945. For almost 55 years, American wars have been fought predominantly on land, and it is anyone's guess as to what the outcome would be if a U.S. naval force were to give battle to an equally modern and well-trained enemy. The nature of modern naval combat may prove to exacerbate the problem of friendly fire. Modern long-range weapons are only effective if an enemy be engaged beyond the visual horizon; this is accomplished by missiles that cannot distinguish a friend from an enemy. Tomahawk strikes can be (and are routinely) ordered against satellite-imaged targets by commanders far removed from the region of conflict. Worse yet, commanding officers of warships and submarines do not have to be informed as to what their Tomahawks are being sent to destroy. The fact that the captain of a combat vessel can be required to release weapons without knowing at what he is shooting should trouble anyone with even a modicum of combat experience. It is not difficult to imagine the ease with which friendly forces ashore can be mistakenly attacked by such "smart" weapons launched blindly from the sea.

The increased accuracy and lethality of today's naval weapons gives a heightened significance to friendly fire in modern naval combat. In World War II, ships that accidentally engaged a friend had a greater probability of missing their target with the opening salvoes. Sometimes it took several minutes to find the range of an opponent; thus, there was more time to realize a mistake and cease fire before any damage was inflicted. Because ships today would rarely be in sight of an enemy during combat, the ability to recognize a friendly fire mistake has dramatically decreased since World War II. In such an engagement, cruise missiles would be launched based on over-the-horizon targeting methods with no possibility of recall if an error was realized. In most cases, there would be little chance of missing the target with these terribly accurate weapons. Even if an urgent radio warning was sent to a mistakenly attacked friend, this ship would still have the extremely difficult task of defeating the missile's sophisticated guidance systems.

With these thoughts in mind, the following are highly recommended:

1. With today's emphasis on littoral warfare, the force separation doctrines currently employed by amphibious forces are crucial to minimizing friendly fire. The fratricide potential is high when hundreds of landing craft, small boats, helicopters, close-air-support aircraft, and surface fire support forces are attempting an opposed assault in a confined coastal area. Have force separation procedures been reviewed and updated since the Persian Gulf War? Can naval surface and air forces supporting a landing electronically identify friendly small boats, landing craft, and troops and vehicles ashore?

2. Staff delinquency has resulted in the worst incidents of friendly fire in history. Staff procedures regarding the control and coordination of forces must be reviewed with a focus on exposing fratricide potential. Commands exercising control of forces in common operational areas should examine how well each communicates the movement and intentions of its units to the others. Additionally, doctrine regarding the separation of submarines from surface and air forces should be reviewed.

3. Final authority to release Tomahawk missiles must be given to the commanding officers of the ships that employ

them. By not allowing a CO to exercise his judgement in this manner, we will remove from the engagement sequence another safeguard against attacking friendly, neutral, or forbidden targets.

4. One objective of every fleet exercise and wargame should be to expose fratricide potential, as even simple engagements can result in friendly fire. Emergent threat response doctrines (such as that in the case of a surprise cruise missile attack) must be reviewed for hidden fratricide dangers. The employment of automatic response weapons such as the Phalanx Close-In Weapon System must be carefully planned and controlled such that they can be allowed to quickly engage targets without endangering surrounding ships and aircraft.

5. The aim of improving operational doctrine should be to balance the freedom to attack effectively against the constraints to safeguard against self-inflicted loss. Collaterally, the objectives of improving tactics should include the creation of standard formations and dispositions that provide for easier discrimination between friends and enemies. Additionally, the effectiveness of visual and electronic recognition procedures should be continually evaluated. Contingency measures must allow for the identification of friendly forces in the cases of restrictive Emissions Control conditions, IFF equipment failure, and a complete electronic blackout.

6. Thoughtful pursuit of IFF technology is highly encouraged. It is difficult to imagine how much greater a role fratricide might have played in World War II if U.S. naval forces did not employ these systems. Despite its benefits, technological efforts to simplify the complexities of modern warfare are, based on past experience, only the beginning of a solution to reducing friendly fire in future conflicts.

VI. LIMITATIONS AND POTENTIAL FOR FUTURE RESEARCH

A. LIMITATIONS

1. Limited Source and Data Availability

The greatest limitation of this study is the unavailability of sources from which reliable data can be extracted. Naval fratricide is a relatively unexplored area of military history, and source material dealing directly with this subject is sparse. Paul Kemp's *Friend or Foe* was relied upon not just because it existed, but because it is extremely well researched and thorough. Despite his focus on the navies of Europe (primarily the Royal Navy), the truths he uncovers appear to apply broadly to all naval forces. His book is very highly recommended.

Naval Chronology is an excellent reference for most U.S. naval fratricide types. However, more research is necessary in order to sort completely the collision data contained therein. Collisions potentially make up as much as 70 percent of all incidents of U.S. naval fratricide in the Second World War. As mentioned previously, war diaries and deck logs maintained by the National Archives and Research Administration may serve an effort to increase the accuracy of the calculations of friendly fire proportions in this study.

2. Sampling Bias

In order for statistical sampling to be most effective, the samples must be randomly drawn from a population.[11] The collisions that were identified as having or not having occurred in combat were drawn from several independent sources and are believed to be independent of one another. However, it is possible that bias exists in the samples from the *Dictionary of American Naval Fighting Ships Online* website. The ship summaries in this source fell into two distinct groups. One group contained many specific details of operations, damage received, and movement of its ships throughout the war. The other group of summaries briefly listed major campaigns and areas of operations with little specific detail concerning damage and its causes. Thus, bias could result from the differences in the way biographers chose to document a ship's life.

Another difficulty with the website is that the summaries of World War II amphibious ships were not available at the time of this study. As such, the sample ratio of combat to non-combat collisions calculated from the 39 classifiable collisions might be accurate only when applied to the total number of collisions of non-amphibious ships. This is not to say that the impact of collisions on friendly fire incidents has been overestimated; it is possible that amphibious ships had a higher rate of combat collisions than their "blue water" counterparts. Again, the only way to be certain of the true proportion of combat collisions is to research and classify all of the 169 incidents of the war.

---

[11] For details regarding the limitations of statistical sampling, confidence intervals, and linear regression, see the applicable sections of Devore and Hamilton.

B. FUTURE RESEARCH

Fratricide research must be ongoing. Continuous study of this problem is the only means by which it can be minimized for future naval forces. Again, technology and doctrine must both be developed with the reduction of friendly fire as a primary objective. As such, the following are suggested as areas of beneficial research into the causes of and solutions to naval friendly fire:

1. An update of *Naval Chronology* is due to be published in November 1999; this will contain revised information resulting from over 55 years of additional research. An overhaul of this thesis using this latest version would give the herein-obtained results greater accuracy.

2. A revision of this thesis could be made by exhaustively researching ships' war diaries and logs contained in the National Archives and Research Administration in College Park, Maryland. If the collision data could be fully separated, they would provide a more accurate calculation of the friendly fire proportion of U.S. naval casualties in World War II. As an additional result, the occurrence of friendly fire in specific types of combat situations could be modeled and tested as a Poisson process.

3. Paul Kemp's *Friend or Foe* is an excellent source primarily because it studies the friendly fire incidents of many navies. Valuable research could be conducted by

comparing U.S. naval fratricide in World War II with that of the Royal Navy and the Kriegsmarine in either this conflict or World War I.

4. Working with the World War II data, there is strong evidence that the potential for naval fratricide is greatest during large-scale amphibious assaults. With the current focus on littoral warfare and power projection ashore, the study of fratricide in amphibious operations throughout history would be extremely valuable.

5. The Falkland Islands War witnessed several incidents of naval fratricide. This conflict took place relatively recently, and its study could provide insight into the role of friendly fire in modern naval combat.

6. A statistical study of friendly fire in naval air forces would be extremely useful. Data from more modern conflicts such as Vietnam and the Falklands War could be studied or compared to that of World War II.

APPENDIX A. FRIENDLY FIRE CHRONOLOGY

ship		date	surface	submarine	air	mine	own wpn		collision
S-26		24 Jan 42							XN
TUCKER	DD 374	04 Aug 42				X			
INGRAHAM	DD 444	22 Aug 42							XN
BUCK	DD 420	22 Aug 42							YN
CHEMUNG	AO 30	22 Aug 42							YN
SAN FRANCISCO	CA 38	30 Sep 42							Y
BREESE	DD 122	30 Sep 42							Y
DUNCAN	DD 485	11 Oct 42	Y						
GRAYSON	DD 435	21 Oct 42							Y
HUGHES	DD 410	25 Oct 42	Y						
HUGHES	DD 410	26 Oct 42							Y
PRESIDENT COOLID	AP 38 (?)	26 Oct 42				X			
SOUTH DAKOTA	BB 57	27 Oct 42							YC
MAHAN	DD 364	27 Oct 42							YC
BUCHANAN	DD 484	12 Nov 42	Y						
AARON WARD	DD 483	13 Nov 42	Y						
O'BANNON	DD 450	13 Nov 42	Y						
ATLANTA	CL 51	13 Nov 42	Y						
FLORENCE NIGHTIN	AP 70	24 Dec 42							Y
THURSTON	AP 77	24 Dec 42							Y
SWORDFISH	SS 193	07 Feb 43			Y				
SC 1024		02 Mar 43							X
MACDONOUGH	DD 351	10 May 43							YC
SICARD	DM 21	10 May 43							YC
LST 6		17 Jun 43							Y
LST 326		17 Jun 43							Y
SC 1330		30 Jun 43							Y
ROE	DD 418	10 Jul 43							YC
SWANSON	DD 443	10 Jul 43							YC
WILLIAM P.BIDDLE	APA 8	10 Jul 43							YC
LST 382		10 Jul 43							YC
LST 345		10 Jul 43							YC
PC 621		10 Jul 43							YC
WOODWORTH	DD 460	13 Jul 43							YC
BUCHANAN	DD 484	13 Jul 43							YC
BRANT	ARS 32	10 Aug 43	Y						
WALLER	DD 466	17 Aug 43							YC
PHILIP	DD 498	17 Aug 43							YC
MONTGOMERY	DM 17	25 Aug 43							YC
PREBLE	DM 20	25 Aug 43							YC
SC 666		13 Sep 43							YC
BRANT	ARS 32	28 Sep 43							Y
PATTERSON	DD 392	29 Sep 43							YN
MCCALLA	DD 488	29 Sep 43							YN
PT 126		30 Sep 43	Y						
O'BANNON	DD 450	06 Oct 43							YC
DORADO	SS 248	12 Oct 43			X				
SPENCE	DD 512	02 Nov 43							YC
NAUTILUS	SS 168	19 Nov 43	Y						
PERKINS	DD 377	29 Nov 43							XN
TAYLOR	DD 468	04 Dec 43	Y						
SMITH	DD 378	01 Jan 44							YN
HUTCHINS	DD 476	01 Jan 44							YN
ST. AUGUSTINE	PG 54	06 Jan 44							XN
PT 110		26 Jan 44							X
PT 114		26 Jan 44							Y
WASHINGTON	BB 56	02 Feb 44							YC
INDIANA	BB 58	02 Feb 44							YC
PT 279		11 Feb 44							X
PILOT	AM 104	18 Feb 44							YN
TULLIBEE	SS 284	26 Mar 44					X	CIRCULAR RUN TORPEDO	
PT 121		27 Mar 44			X				
PT 353		27 Mar 44			X				
TUNNY	SS 282	30 Mar 44			Y				
ATR 98		12 Apr 44							X
PT 346		29 Apr 44			X				
PT 347		29 Apr 44			X				

ship			date	surface		submarine		air	mine	own wpn		collision
PARROTT	DD 218		02 May 44									YN
PHILADELPHIA	CL 41		23 May 44									YC
LAUB	DD 613		23 May 44									YC
LST 375			06 Jun 44									YC
PHEASANT	AM 61		07 Jun 44									Y
LST 84			17 Jun 44	Y								
HUDSON	DD 475		19 Jun 44	Y								
VALOR	AMC 108		29 Jun 44									X
PGM 7			18 Jul 44									Y
NOA	APD 24		12 Sep 44									XN
FULLAM	DD 474		12 Sep 44									YN
FORREST	DD 461		01 Oct 44									Y
SEAWOLF	SS 197		03 Oct 44	X								
PRICHETT	DD 561		12 Oct 44	Y								
COWELL	DD 547		14 Oct 44									Y
WARHAWK	AP 168		21 Oct 44									Y
TANG	SS 306		24 Oct 44							X		
											CIRCULAR RUN TORPEDO	
ATR 1			06 Dec 44									Y
SARGENT BAY	CVE 83		03 Jan 45									Y
ROBERT F. KELLER	DE 419		03 Jan 45									Y
MONADNOCK	CM 9		03 Jan 45									Y
BELL	DD 587		04 Jan 45									Y
EDWIN A. HOWARD	DE 346		05 Jan 45									Y
NEWCOMB	DD 586		06 Jan 45	Y								
LOWRY	DD 770		06 Jan 45	Y								
COLORADO	BB 45		09 Jan 45	Y								
GUADALUPE	AO 32		09 Jan 45									Y
CLEMSON	APD 31		10 Jan 45									Y
LATIMER	APA 152		10 Jan 45									Y
LST 567			10 Jan 45									Y
LST 700			11 Jan 45	Y								
LST 710			12 Jan 45	Y								
LST 778			12 Jan 45	Y								
LST 710			18 Jan 45									Y
LST 752			18 Jan 45									Y
EXTRACTOR	ARS 15		24 Jan 45			X						
PT 77			01 Feb 45	X								
PT 79			01 Feb 45	X								
TAKELMA	ATF 113		11 Feb 45									Y
INGRAHAM	DD 694		16 Feb 45									Y
BARTON	DD 722		16 Feb 45									Y
CHESTER	CA 27		19 Feb 45									Y
BRADFORD	DD 545		19 Feb 45									Y
FINNEGAN	DE 307		19 Feb 45									Y
BILOXI	CL 80		20 Feb 45	Y								
SAMARITAN	AH 10		20 Feb 45	Y								
NAPA	APA 157		20 Feb 45									Y
LOGAN	APA 196		20 Feb 45									Y
STARR	AKA 67		20 Feb 45									Y
WILLIAMSON	DD 244		21 Feb 45									YN
YANCEY	AKA 93		21 Feb 45									Y
LST 390			21 Feb 45									Y
MELVIN R. NAWMAN	DE 416		22 Feb 45									Y
PC 877			23 Feb 45									Y
HEYWOOD L. EDWARDS	DD 663		24 Feb 45									Y
BRYANT	DD 665		24 Feb 45									Y
PC 578			24 Feb 45									Y
FAYETTE	APA 43		25 Feb 45									Y
MULIPHEN	AKA 61		25 Feb 45									Y
HAMLIN	AV 15		25 Feb 45	Y								
LST 928			25 Feb 45									Y
LST 121			26 Feb 45									Y
SAN JACINTO	CVL 30		27 Feb 45									Y
COLHOUN	DD 801		27 Feb 45									Y
MERRIMACK	AO 37		27 Feb 45									Y
PRESIDENT ADAMS	APA 19		27 Feb 45									Y
KNOX	APA 46		27 Feb 45									Y
TOLLAND	AKA 64		27 Feb 45									Y
LST 779			27 Feb 45									Y
LST 809			27 Feb 45									Y
PCS 1461			28 Feb 45									Y

ship		date	surface	submarine	air	mine	own wpn	collision
WHITLEY	AKA 91	28 Feb 45						Y
LST 641		28 Feb 45						Y
LST 787		28 Feb 45						Y
BERRIEN	APA 62	01 Mar 45						Y
STOKES	AKA 68	02 Mar 45						Y
LST 224		02 Mar 45						Y
LST 247		02 Mar 45						Y
LST 634		02 Mar 45						Y
LST 642		05 Mar 45						Y
INTREPID	CV 11	18 Mar 45	Y					
ESSEX	CV 9	19 Mar 45	Y					
ENTERPRISE	CV 6	20 Mar 45	Y					
HERCULES	AK 41	20 Mar 45						Y
SEDERSTROM	DE 31	25 Mar 45						Y
AGENOR	ARL 3	28 Mar 45						Y
ROPER	APD 20	30 Mar 45						Y
PENSACOLA	CA 24	31 Mar 45						Y
COOS BAY	AVP 25	31 Mar 45						Y
FRANKS	DD 554	02 Apr 45						Y
BORIE	DD 704	02 Apr 45						Y
LACERTA	AKA 29	02 Apr 45	Y					
NORMAN SCOTT	DD 690	04 Apr 45						Y
LST 399		04 Apr 45						Y
THORNTON	AVD 11	05 Apr 45						YN
ASHTABULA	AO 51	05 Apr 45						YN
ESCALANTE	AO 70	05 Apr 45						YN
AGENOR	ARL 3	05 Apr 45						YN
LST 273		05 Apr 45						Y
LST 646		05 Apr 45						Y
LST 810		05 Apr 45						Y
LST 940		05 Apr 45						Y
LST 1000		05 Apr 45						Y
NORTH CAROLINA	BB 55	06 Apr 45	Y					
PASADENA	CL 65	06 Apr 45	Y					
PCS 1390		06 Apr 45	Y					
BARNETT	APA 5	06 Apr 45	Y					
DANIEL T. GRIFFIN	APD 38	06 Apr 45						Y
LEO	AKA 60	06 Apr 45	Y					
LST 241		06 Apr 45	Y					
LST 1000		06 Apr 45	Y					
AUDRAIN	APA 59	07 Apr 45	Y					
LST 890		07 Apr 45						Y
LST 939		08 Apr 45						Y
PORTERFIELD	DD 682	09 Apr 45	Y					
YMS 96		10 Apr 45						Y
TRATHEN	DD 520	11 Apr 45	Y					
BERRIEN	APA 62	11 Apr 45						Y
LEO	AKA 60	11 Apr 45	Y					
NEW MEXICO	BB 40	12 Apr 45	Y					
WABASH	AOG 4	12 Apr 45						Y
WYANDOT	AKA 92	12 Apr 45						Y
LST 241		14 Apr 45						Y
MCDERMUT	DD 677	16 Apr 45	Y					
BENHAM	DD 796	17 Apr 45	Y					
LST 929		18 Apr 45						Y
FLUSSER	DD368	22 Apr 45						Y
WINOOSKI	AO 38	22 Apr 45						Y
STEAMER BAY	CVE 87	25 Apr 45						Y
HALE	DD 642	25 Apr 45						Y
WILLIAM D. PORTER	DD 579	27 Apr 45	Y					
LANG	DD 399	28 Apr 45						Y
HUDSON	DD 475	04 May 45						Y
YMS 311		04 May 45	Y					
YMS 327		04 May 45	Y					
WICHITA	CA 45	12 May 45	Y					
BATAAN	CVL 29	13 May 45	Y					
SHIPLEY BAY	CVE 85	16 May 45						Y
VAMMEN	DE 644	19 May 45						Y
HEYWOOD L. EDWA	DD 663	24 May 45	Y					
COWELL	DD 547	25 May 45	Y					
DYSON	DD 572	05 Jun 45						Y

ship			date	surface		submarine		air	mine	own wpn		collision
BEALE		DD 471	06 Jun 45									Y
REQUISITE		AM 109	06 Jun 45									Y
SPEAR		AM 322	06 Jun 45									Y
YAHARA		AOG 37	06 Jun 45									Y
VICKSBURG		CL 86	11 Jun 45									Y
LINDENWALD		LSD 6	11 Jun 45	Y								
PGM 24			14 Jun 45									Y
O'FLAHERTY		DE 340	15 Jun 45									Y
CHESTATEE		AOG 49	17 Jun 45									Y
YAKUTAT		AVP 32	18 Jun 45									Y
DEVICE		AM220	19 Jun 45									Y
DOUR		AM223	19 Jun 45									Y
LST 562			19 Jun 45									Y
NEUENDORF		DE 200	24 Jun 45									Y
YMS 339			24 Jun 45					Y				
SUISUN		AVP 53	26 Jun 45									Y
ASHTABULA		AO 51	03 Jul 45									Y
FLUSSER		DD 368	15 Jul 45									Y
THOMAS E. FRASER		DM 24	15 Jul 45									Y
GANYMEDE		AK 104	27 Jul 45									Y
BANCROFT		DD 598	31 Jul 45									Y
SEMINOLE		AKA 104	03 Aug 45									Y
BRISTOL		DD 857	05 Aug 45									YN
JOHN W. WEEKS		DD 701	09 Aug 45	Y								
			X	3		1		5	2	2		10
			Y	49		0		3	0	0		158
			Total	52		1		8	2	2		168

											XN	5
Proportions against all types				October 1944 - August 1945							XC	0
	surface	0.32				number of surface incidents		40			YN	15
	submarine	0.01				proportion of total surface incidents		0.77			YC	24
	air	0.05									Total	44
	mine	0.01				number of combat collisions		69				
	own weapon	0.01				proportion of total combat collisions		0.71				
	collision	0.60										

Legend			
	X	Lost	
	Y	Damaged	
	C*	Combat-related	
	N*	Not combat-related	

* Used to separate collision data; only combat-related collisions are considered friendly fire.

APPENDIX B. FRIENDLY FIRE CHRONOLOGY - LARGE SHIPS

ship		date	surface		submarine		air	mine	own wpn		collision
CHEMUNG	AO 30	22 Aug 42									YN
SAN FRANCISCO	CA 38	30 Sep 42									Y
PRESIDENT COOLIDGE	AP 38 (?)	26 Oct 42						X			
SOUTH DAKOTA	BB 57	27 Oct 42									YC
ATLANTA	CL 51	13 Nov 42	Y								
FLORENCE NIGHTINGALE	AP 70	24 Dec 42									Y
THURSTON	AP 77	24 Dec 42									Y
WILLIAM P.BIDDLE	APA 8	10 Jul 43									Y
WASHINGTON	BB 56	02 Feb 44									YC
INDIANA	BB 58	02 Feb 44									YC
PHILADELPHIA	CL 41	23 May 44									YC
WARHAWK	AP 168	21 Oct 44									Y
SARGENT BAY	CVE 83	03 Jan 45									Y
COLORADO	BB 45	09 Jan 45	Y								
GUADALUPE	AO 32	09 Jan 45									Y
LATIMER	APA 152	10 Jan 45									Y
CHESTER	CA 27	19 Feb 45									Y
BILOXI	CL 80	20 Feb 45	Y								
SAMARITAN	AH 10	20 Feb 45	Y								
NAPA	APA 157	20 Feb 45									Y
LOGAN	APA 196	20 Feb 46									Y
STARR	AKA 67	20 Feb 45									Y
YANCEY	AKA 93	21 Feb 45									Y
FAYETTE	APA 43	25 Feb 45									Y
MULIPHEN	AKA 61	25 Feb 45									Y
HAMLIN	AV 15	25 Feb 45	Y								
SAN JACINTO	CVL 30	27 Feb 45									Y
MERRIMACK	AO 37	27 Feb 45									Y
PRESIDENT ADAMS	APA 19	27 Feb 45									Y
KNOX	APA 46	27 Feb 45									Y
TOLLAND	AKA 64	27 Feb 45									Y
WHITLEY	AKA 91	28 Feb 45									Y
STOKES	AKA 68	02 Mar 45									Y
INTREPID	CV 11	18 Mar 45	Y								
ESSEX	CV 9	19 Mar 45	Y								
ENTERPRISE	CV 6	20 Mar 45	Y								
HERCULES	AK 41	20 Mar 45									Y
PENSACOLA	CA 24	31 Mar 45									Y
LACERTA	AKA 29	02 Apr 45	Y								
ASHTABULA	AO 51	05 Apr 45									YN
ESCALANTE	AO 70	05 Apr 45									YN
NORTH CAROLINA	BB 55	06 Apr 45	Y								
PASADENA	CL 65	06 Apr 45	Y								
BARNETT	APA 5	06 Apr 45	Y								
LEO	AKA 60	06 Apr 45	Y								
AUDRAIN	APA 59	07 Apr 45	Y								
BERRIEN	APA 62	11 Apr 45									Y
LEO	AKA 60	11 Apr 45	Y								
NEW MEXICO	BB 40	12 Apr 45	Y								
WYANDOT	AKA 92	12 Apr 45									Y
WINOOSKI	AO 38	22 Apr 45									Y
STEAMER BAY	CVE 87	25 Apr 45									Y

ship		date	surface		submarine		air	mine	own wpn		collision
WICHITA	CA 45	12 May 45	Y								
BATAAN	CVL 29	13 May 45	Y								
SHIPLEY BAY	CVE 85	16 May 45									Y
VICKSBURG	CL 86	11 Jun 45									Y
ASHTABULA	AO 51	03 Jul 45									Y
GANYMEDE	AK 104	27 Jul 45									Y
SEMINOLE	AKA 104	03 Aug 45									Y
			X	0		0	0	1	0		0
			Y	18		0	0	0	0		40
			Total	18		0	0	1	0		40

Proportions against all types			October 1944 - August 1945				Combat collisions this group				
surface	0.41		number of surface incidents	17			p * Y(collisions)	25			
collisions	0.56		proportion of total group surface incidents	0.94							
other	0.02										
			number of combat collisions	19							
			proportion of total group combat collisions	0.78							

APPENDIX C.   FRIENDLY FIRE CHRONOLOGY - SMALL SHIPS

ship		date	surface		submarine		air	mine	own wpn		collision
TUCKER	DD 374	04 Aug 42						X			
INGRAHAM	DD 444	22 Aug 42									XN
BUCK	DD 420	22 Aug 42									YN
BREESE	DD 122	30 Sep 42									Y
DUNCAN	DD 485	11 Oct 42	Y								
GRAYSON	DD 435	21 Oct 42									Y
HUGHES	DD 410	25 Oct 42	Y								
HUGHES	DD 410	26 Oct 42									Y
MAHAN	DD 364	27 Oct 42									YC
BUCHANAN	DD 484	12 Nov 42	Y								
AARON WARD	DD 483	13 Nov 42	Y								
O'BANNON	DD 450	13 Nov 42	Y								
SC 1024		02 Mar 43									X
MACDONOUGH	DD 351	10 May 43									YC
SICARD	DM 21	10 May 43									YC
LST 6		17 Jun 43									Y
LST 326		17 Jun 43									Y
SC 1330		30 Jun 43									Y
ROE	DD 418	10 Jul 43									YC
SWANSON	DD 443	10 Jul 43									YC
PC 621		10 Jul 43									YC
LST 382		10 Jul 43									YC
LST 345		10 Jul 43									YC
WOODWORTH	DD 460	13 Jul 43									YC
BUCHANAN	DD 484	13 Jul 43									YC
BRANT	ARS 32	10 Aug 43	Y								
WALLER	DD 466	17 Aug 43									YC
PHILIP	DD 498	17 Aug 43									YC
MONTGOMERY	DM 17	25 Aug 43									YC
PREBLE	DM 20	25 Aug 43									YC
SC 666		13 Sep 43									YC
BRANT	ARS 32	28 Sep 43									Y
PATTERSON	DD 392	29 Sep 43									YN
MCCALLA	DD 488	29 Sep 43									YN
PT 126		30 Sep 43	Y								
O'BANNON	DD 450	06 Oct 43									YC
SPENCE	DD 512	02 Nov 43									YC
PERKINS	DD 377	29 Nov 43									XN
TAYLOR	DD 468	04 Dec 43	Y								
SMITH	DD 378	01 Jan 44									YN
HUTCHINS	DD 476	01 Jan 44									YN
ST. AUGUSTINE	PG 54	06 Jan 44									XN
PT 110		26 Jan 44									X
PT 114		26 Jan 44									Y
PT 279		11 Feb 44									X
PILOT	AM 104	18 Feb 44									YN
PT 121		27 Mar 44					X				
PT 353		27 Mar 44					X				
ATR 98		12 Apr 44									X
PT 346		29 Apr 44					X				
PT 347		29 Apr 44					X				
PARROTT	DD 218	02 May 44									YN
LAUB	DD 613	23 May 44									YC
LST 375		06 Jun 44									YC
PHEASANT	AM 61	07 Jun 44									Y
LST 84		17 Jun 44	Y								
HUDSON	DD 475	19 Jun 44	Y								
VALOR	AMC 108	29 Jun 44									X
PGM 7		18 Jul 44									Y
NOA	APD 24	12 Sep 44									XN
FULLAM	DD 474	12 Sep 44									YN
FORREST	DD 461	01 Oct 44									Y
PRICHETT	DD 561	12 Oct 44	Y								
COWELL	DD 547	14 Oct 44									Y
WARHAWK	AP 168	21 Oct 44									Y
ATR 1		06 Dec 44									Y
ROBERT F. KELLER	DE 419	03 Jan 45									Y
MONADNOCK	CM 9	03 Jan 45									Y
BELL	DD 587	04 Jan 45									Y
EDWIN A. HOWARD	DE 346	05 Jan 45									Y
NEWCOMB	DD 586	06 Jan 45	Y								

ship		date	surface		submarine		air	mine	own wpn		collision
LOWRY	DD 770	06 Jan 45	Y								
CLEMSON	APD 31	10 Jan 45									Y
LST 567		10 Jan 45									Y
LST 700		11 Jan 45	Y								
LST 710		12 Jan 45	Y								
LST 778		12 Jan 45	Y								
LST 710		18 Jan 45									Y
LST 752		18 Jan 45									Y
EXTRACTOR	ARS 15	24 Jan 45			X						
PT 77		01 Feb 45	X								
PT 79		01 Feb 45	X								
TAKELMA	ATF 113	11 Feb 45									Y
INGRAHAM	DD 694	16 Feb 45									Y
BARTON	DD 722	16 Feb 45									Y
BRADFORD	DD 545	19 Feb 45									Y
FINNEGAN	DE 307	19 Feb 45									Y
WILLIAMSON	DD 244	21 Feb 45									YN
LST 390		21 Feb 45									Y
MELVIN R. NAWMAN	DE 416	22 Feb 45									Y
PC 877		23 Feb 45									Y
HEYWOOD L. EDWARDS	DD 663	24 Feb 45									Y
BRYANT	DD 665	24 Feb 45									Y
PC 578		24 Feb 45									Y
LST 928		25 Feb 45									Y
LST 121		26 Feb 45									Y
COLHOUN	DD 801	27 Feb 45									Y
LST 779		27 Feb 45									Y
LST 809		27 Feb 45									Y
PCS 1461		28 Feb 45									Y
LST 641		28 Feb 45									Y
LST 787		28 Feb 45									Y
LST 224		02 Mar 45									Y
LST 247		02 Mar 45									Y
LST 634		02 Mar 45									Y
LST 642		05 Mar 45									Y
BERRIEN	APA 62	01 Mar 45									Y
SEDERSTROM	DE 31	25 Mar 45									Y
ROPER	APD 20	30 Mar 45									Y
COOS BAY	AVP 25	31 Mar 45									Y
FRANKS	DD 554	02 Apr 45									Y
BORIE	DD 704	02 Apr 45									Y
NORMAN SCOTT	DD 690	04 Apr 45									Y
LST 399		04 Apr 45									Y
AGENOR	ARL 3	05 Apr 45									YN
THORNTON	AVD 11	05 Apr 45									YN
LST 273		05 Apr 45									Y
LST 646		05 Apr 45									Y
LST 810		05 Apr 45									Y
LST 940		05 Apr 45									Y
LST 1000		05 Apr 45									Y
DANIEL T. GRIFFIN	APD 38	06 Apr 45									Y
PCS 1390		06 Apr 45	Y								
LST 241		06 Apr 45	Y								
LST 1000		06 Apr 45	Y								
LST 890		07 Apr 45									Y
LST 939		08 Apr 45									Y
PORTERFIELD	DD 682	09 Apr 45	Y								
YMS 96		10 Apr 45									Y
TRATHEN	DD 520	11 Apr 45	Y								
WABASH	AOG 4	12 Apr 45									Y
LST 241		14 Apr 45									Y
MCDERMUT	DD 677	16 Apr 45	Y								
BENHAM	DD 796	17 Apr 45	Y								
LST 929		18 Apr 45									Y
FLUSSER	DD368	22 Apr 45									Y
HALE	DD 642	25 Apr 45									Y
WILLIAM D. PORTER	DD 579	27 Apr 45	Y								
LANG	DD 399	28 Apr 45									Y
HUDSON	DD 475	04 May 45									Y
YMS 311		04 May 45	Y								
YMS 327		04 May 45	Y								
VAMMEN	DE 644	19 May 45									Y

68

ship		date	surface		submarine		air	mine	own wpn		collision
REQUISITE	AM 109	06 Jun 45									Y
SPEAR	AM 322	06 Jun 45									Y
YAHARA	AOG 37	06 Jun 45									Y
LINDENWALD	LSD 6	11 Jun 45	Y								
PGM 24		14 Jun 45									Y
CHESTATEE	AOG 49	17 Jun 45									Y
YAKUTAT	AVP 32	18 Jun 45									Y
DEVICE	AM220	19 Jun 45									Y
DOUR	AM223	19 Jun 45									Y
LST 562		19 Jun 45									Y
NEUENDORF	DE 200	24 Jun 45									Y
YMS 339		24 Jun 45					Y				
SUISUN	AVP 53	26 Jun 45									Y
FLUSSER	DD 368	15 Jul 45									Y
THOMAS E. FRASER	DM 24	15 Jul 45									Y
BANCROFT	DD 598	31 Jul 45									Y
BRISTOL	DD 857	05 Aug 45									YN
JOHN W. WEEKS	DD 701	09 Aug 45	Y								
			X	2		1	4	1	0		9
			Y	30		0	1	0	0		118
			Total	32		1	5	1	0		127

Proportions against all types			October 1944 - August 1945						Combat collisions this group		
surface	0.29			number of surface incidents			22		p * Y(collisions)		73
collisions	0.65			proportion of total group combat collisions			0.69				
air	0.04										
other	0.02			number of combat collisions			49				
				proportion of total group combat collisions			0.68				

APPENDIX D. FRIENDLY FIRE CHRONOLOGY - AMPHIBIOUS SHIPS

ship			date	surface		submarine		air	mine	own wpn		collision
LST 6			17 Jun 43									Y
LST 326			17 Jun 43									Y
WILLIAM P.BIDDLE	APA 8		10 Jul 43									YC
LST 382			10 Jul 43									YC
LST 345			10 Jul 43									YC
LST 375			06 Jun 44									YC
LST 84			17 Jun 44	Y								
NOA	APD 24		12 Sep 44									XN
CLEMSON	APD 31		10 Jan 45									Y
LATIMER	APA 152		10 Jan 45									Y
LST 567			10 Jan 45									Y
LST 700			11 Jan 45	Y								
LST 710			12 Jan 45	Y								
LST 778			12 Jan 45	Y								
LST 710			18 Jan 45									Y
LST 752			18 Jan 45									Y
NAPA	APA 157		20 Feb 45									Y
LOGAN	APA 196		20 Feb 45									Y
STARR	AKA 67		20 Feb 45									Y
YANCEY	AKA 93		21 Feb 45									Y
LST 390			21 Feb 45									Y
FAYETTE	APA 43		25 Feb 45									Y
MULIPHEN	AKA 61		25 Feb 45									Y
LST 928			25 Feb 45									Y
LST 121			26 Feb 45									Y
PRESIDENT ADAMS	APA 19		27 Feb 45									Y
KNOX	APA 46		27 Feb 45									Y
TOLLAND	AKA 64		27 Feb 45									Y
LST 779			27 Feb 45									Y
LST 809			27 Feb 45									Y
WHITLEY	AKA 91		28 Feb 45									Y
LST 641			28 Feb 45									Y
LST 787			28 Feb 45									Y
BERRIEN	APA 62		01 Mar 45									Y
STOKES	AKA 68		02 Mar 45									Y
LST 224			02 Mar 45									Y
LST 247			02 Mar 45									Y
LST 634			02 Mar 45									Y
LST 642			05 Mar 45									Y
ROPER	APD 20		30 Mar 45									Y
LACERTA	AKA 29		02 Apr 45	Y								
LST 399			04 Apr 45									Y
LST 273			05 Apr 45									Y
LST 646			05 Apr 45									Y
LST 810			05 Apr 45									Y
LST 940			05 Apr 45									Y
LST 1000			05 Apr 45									Y
BARNETT	APA 5		06 Apr 45	Y								
DANIEL T. GRIFFIN	APD 38		06 Apr 45									Y
LEO	AKA 60		06 Apr 45	Y								
LST 241			06 Apr 45	Y								
LST 1000			06 Apr 45	Y								
AUDRAIN	APA 59		07 Apr 45	Y								
LST 890			07 Apr 45									Y
LST 939			08 Apr 45									Y
BERRIEN	APA 62		11 Apr 45									Y
LEO	AKA 60		11 Apr 45	Y								

ship			date	surface		submarine		air	mine	own wpn		collision
WYANDOT		AKA 92	12 Apr 45									Y
LST 241			14 Apr 45									Y
LST 929			18 Apr 45									Y
LST 562			19 Jun 45									Y
SEMINOLE		AKA 104	03 Aug 45									Y
			X	0		0		0	0	0		1
			Y	11		0		0	0	0		50
			Total	11		0		0	0	0		51

Proportions against all types			October 1944 - August 1945				Combat collisions this group	
	surface	0.26	number of surface incidents	10		p * Y(collisions)	31
	collisions	0.74	proportion of total group surface incidents	0.91			
			number of combat collisions	27			
			proportion of total group combat collisions	0.88			

APPENDIX E. FRIENDLY FIRE CHRONOLOGY - SUBMARINES

ship			date	surface		submarine		air	mine	own wpn		collision
U.S.												
SWORDFISH	SS 193		07 Feb 43					Y				
DORADO	SS 248		12 Oct 43					X				
NAUTILUS	SS 168		19 Nov 43	Y								
TULLIBEE	SS 284		26 Apr 44							X	CIRCULAR RUN TORPEDO	
TUNNY	SS 282		30 Mar 44					Y				
SEAWOLF	SS 197		03 Oct 44	X								
TANG	SS 306		24 Oct 44							X	CIRCULAR RUN TORPEDO	
			X	1		0		1	0	2		0
			Y	1		0		2	0	0		0
			Total	2		0		3	0	2		0

Friendly fire impact

war losses	52	
friendly fire losses	4	
proportion	0.08	

Own weapon impact

own weapon losses	2
proportion of total losses	0.50

ship		date	surface	submarine	air	mine	own wpn		collision
U Boats - WW I									
U13		12 Aug 14				X			
U7		21 Jan 15		X					
UC2		02 Jul 15					X	MINE	
UC9		21 Oct 15					X	MINE	
UC12		16 Mar 15					X	MINE	
UC32		23 Feb 17					X	MINE	
UC68		13 Mar 17					X	MINE	
U59		14 May 17				X			
UC36		May 1917					X	MINE	
UC44		04 Aug 17				X			
UC42		10 Sep 17					X	MINE	
UB41		05 Oct 17				X			
UB119		May 1918				X			
UC11		26 Jun 18				X			
UB65		10 Jul 18					X	TORPEDO	
		Total	0	1	0	6	8		0

ship		date	surface	submarine	air	mine	own wpn		collision
U Boats - WW II									
U15		01 Feb 40	X						
U25		03 Aug 40					X	MINE	
U557		16 Dec 41							X
U133		14 Mar 42				X			
U585		30 Mar 42				X			
U254		08 Dec 42							X
U439		04 May 43							X
U659		04 May 43							X
U377		15 Jan 44					X	TORPEDO	
U455		06 Apr 44				X			
U235		14 Apr 45	X						
		Total	2	0	0	4	2		4

	WW I	WW II
Friendly fire impact		
war losses	178	784
friendly fire losses	15	12
proportion	0.08	0.015
Own weapon impact		
own weapon losses	8	2
proportion of total losses	0.53	0.17

Estimated proportion of friendly combat collisions					Friendly fire impact					
						War Totals				
p = YC / (YC + YN)	0.62					Lost	226			
						Damaged	993			
Estimated number of combat-related collisions						Total	1219			
p * Y(collisions)	97									
						Friendly Fire Totals		min	max	
						Lost	13			
90% CI on p (with FPC)**						Damaged	149	132	167	
lower bound	0.50					Total	162	145	180	
upper bound	0.73									
						Proportions		min	max	
						Lost	0.06			
						Damaged	0.15	0.13	0.17	
						Total	0.13	0.12	0.15	
** Interval (0.46, 0.70) contains true value of p with 90% probability.										

p   = estimated proportion of friendly combat collisions of total
      population
YC = number of friendly combat collisions sampled
YN = number of non-combat collisions sampled

Y(collisions) = number of collisions causing damage (total population)
              = 158

n = number of samples
  = 39
N = population size
  = 158

FPC = Finite Population Correction
    = $[1 - (n/N)]^{1/2}$

q = 1 - p
α = 0.10   (1 - 90%)
$z_{\alpha/2}$ = 1.645   (from standard normal distribution)

lower bound = $p - (z_{\alpha/2}) * (pq/n)^{1/2} * FPC$
upper bound = $p + (z_{\alpha/2}) * (pq/n)^{1/2} * FPC$

minimum friendly fire damaged = lower bound * total incidents of damage
maximum friendly fire damaged = upper bound * total incidents of damage

minimum proportion damaged = proportion (minimum ff damaged) / 993
maximum proportion damaged = proportion (maximum ff damaged) / 993

APPENDIX G.   MONTHLY CASUALTY TOTALS

year	month	loss	damage	total	collisions	diff	friendly fire				
1941	o	1	2	3							
	n										
	d	10	16	26							
1942	j		3	3							
	f	4	6	10							
	m	6		6							
	a	1		1							
	m	9	5	14							
	j	2	1	3							
	j										
	a	8	10	18	2	1	1				
	s	3	5	8	2						
	o	5	17	22	4	3	3				
	n	11	29	40		4	4				
	d	1	3	4	2						
1943	j	2	2	4							
	f	1		1		1	1				
	m		2	2							
	a	1	2	3							
	m		4	4	2						
	j		9	9	3						
	j	5	14	19	8						
	a		10	10	4	1	1				
	s	2	17	19	4	1	1				
	o	4	7	11	1	1	1				
	n	5	16	21	1	1	1				
	d	2	13	15		1	1				
1944	j	2	13	15	3						
	f		15	15	3						
	m	1	4	5		4	4				
	a	2	5	7		2	2				
	m	4	9	13	3						
	j	6	45	51	2	2	2				
	j	1	8	9	1						
	a	1	4	5							
	s	3	4	7	1						
	o	9	57	66	3	3	3				
	n	2	23	25							
	d	7	46	53	1						
1945	j	6	68	74	11	7	7				
	f	2	71	73	33	5	5				
	m	2	55	57	12	3	3				
	a	16	186	202	27	16	16				
	m	18	77	95	3	6	6				
	j	5	84	89	15	2	2				
	j	4	17	21	5						
	a		9	9	2	1	1				
	ships	174									
	subs	52									
	total	226	993	1219			65				

APPENDIX H. REGRESSION ESTIMATES OF MONTHLY FRIENDLY FIRE TOTALS

year	month	cut	uncut	sqrtCut	sqrtUncut	3rtCut	3rtUncut	4rtCut	4rtUncut	mixCut	mixUncut
1941	o	0.35	0.13	0.38	0.17	0.29	0.11	0.20	0.07	0.26	0.19
	n	-0.11	-0.33	0.00	0.06	0.00	-0.03	0.00	0.02	0.72	0.74
	d	3.82	3.63	3.36	2.87	3.01	2.30	2.72	1.83	3.74	3.24
1942	j	0.35	0.13	0.38	0.17	0.29	0.11	0.20	0.07	0.26	0.19
	f	1.40	1.20	1.28	0.92	1.08	0.67	0.90	0.49	1.38	1.15
	m	0.80	0.59	0.77	0.48	0.62	0.33	0.48	0.23	0.74	0.60
	a	0.04	-0.17	0.12	0.02	0.08	0.01	0.05	0.01	0.01	0.00
	m	2.01	1.80	1.80	1.39	1.56	1.05	1.33	0.79	2.00	1.70
	j	0.35	0.13	0.38	0.17	0.29	0.11	0.20	0.07	0.26	0.19
	j	-0.11	-0.33	0.00	0.06	0.00	-0.03	0.00	0.02	0.72	0.74
	a	2.61	2.41	2.32	1.88	2.04	1.45	1.78	1.11	2.60	2.23
	s	1.10	0.89	1.03	0.70	0.85	0.49	0.69	0.35	1.06	0.88
	o	3.21	3.02	2.84	2.37	2.52	1.87	2.25	1.46	3.18	2.74
	n	5.93	5.76	5.19	4.66	4.74	3.88	4.44	3.20	5.59	4.88
	d	0.50	0.28	0.51	0.27	0.40	0.18	0.29	0.12	0.41	0.32
1943	j	0.50	0.28	0.51	0.27	0.40	0.18	0.29	0.12	0.41	0.32
	f	0.04	-0.17	0.12	0.02	0.08	0.01	0.05	0.01	0.01	0.00
	m	0.19	-0.02	0.25	0.09	0.18	0.06	0.12	0.04	0.11	0.07
	a	0.35	0.13	0.38	0.17	0.29	0.11	0.20	0.07	0.26	0.19
	m	0.50	0.28	0.51	0.27	0.40	0.18	0.29	0.12	0.41	0.32
	j	1.25	1.04	1.16	0.81	0.97	0.58	0.79	0.42	1.22	1.02
	j	2.76	2.56	2.45	2.00	2.16	1.55	1.90	1.20	2.75	2.36
	a	1.40	1.20	1.28	0.92	1.08	0.67	0.90	0.49	1.38	1.15
	s	2.76	2.56	2.45	2.00	2.16	1.55	1.90	1.20	2.75	2.36
	o	1.55	1.35	1.41	1.04	1.20	0.76	1.00	0.56	1.54	1.29
	n	3.06	2.87	2.71	2.25	2.40	1.76	2.13	1.37	3.04	2.61
	d	2.16	1.96	1.93	1.51	1.68	1.15	1.44	0.87	2.16	1.83
1944	j	2.16	1.96	1.93	1.51	1.68	1.15	1.44	0.87	2.16	1.83
	f	2.16	1.96	1.93	1.51	1.68	1.15	1.44	0.87	2.16	1.83
	m	0.65	0.43	0.64	0.37	0.51	0.25	0.39	0.17	0.57	0.46
	a	0.95	0.74	0.90	0.58	0.73	0.41	0.58	0.29	0.90	0.74
	m	1.85	1.65	1.67	1.27	1.44	0.95	1.22	0.71	1.85	1.56
	j	7.59	7.43	6.62	6.10	6.12	5.19	5.83	4.36	6.95	6.09
	j	1.25	1.04	1.16	0.81	0.97	0.58	0.79	0.42	1.22	1.02
	a	0.65	0.43	0.64	0.37	0.51	0.25	0.39	0.17	0.57	0.46
	s	0.95	0.74	0.90	0.58	0.73	0.41	0.58	0.29	0.90	0.74
	o	9.86	9.72	8.58	8.08	8.01	7.02	7.77	6.01	8.69	7.65
	n	3.67	3.48	3.23	2.75	2.89	2.19	2.61	1.73	3.60	3.11
	d	7.89	7.74	6.88	6.36	6.37	5.43	6.09	4.57	7.18	6.31
1945	j	11.06	10.93	9.62	9.14	9.03	8.01	8.83	6.93	9.58	8.45
	f	10.91	10.78	9.49	9.01	8.90	7.89	8.69	6.81	9.47	8.36
	m	8.50	8.35	7.40	6.89	6.88	5.91	6.61	5.01	7.66	6.73
	a	30.39	30.41	26.33	26.54	25.53	24.93	26.45	23.11	21.75	19.40
	m	14.23	14.13	12.36	11.95	11.71	10.68	11.63	9.40	11.82	10.46
	j	13.33	13.22	11.58	11.15	10.94	9.91	10.82	8.68	11.20	9.90
	j	3.06	2.87	2.71	2.25	2.40	1.76	2.13	1.37	3.04	2.61
	a	1.25	1.04	1.16	0.81	0.97	0.58	0.79	0.42	1.22	1.02
	Total	171.12	162.23	151.28	135.59	138.71	115.66	131.67	98.48	151.48	132.02
	% ff	0.140	0.133	0.124	0.111	0.114	0.095	0.108	0.081	0.124	0.108

LIST OF REFERENCES

Brown, David. *Warship Losses of World War Two*. 1990. Annapolis: Naval Institute Press, 1995.

Cochran, William. *Sampling Techniques*. Third ed. New York: John Wiley & Sons, 1977.

Cremer, Peter E. *U-Boat Commander*. 1982. Annapolis: Naval Institute Press, 1984.

Devore, Jay L. *Probability and Statistics for Engineering and the Sciences*. Fourth ed. Pacific Grove, CA: Brooks/Cole, 1995.

Gauker, Eleanor, and Christopher Blood. "Friendly Fire Incidents during World War II Naval Operations." *Naval War College Review* XLVIII, No. 1 (1995): 115-122.

Hamilton, Lawrence C. *Regression with Graphics: A Second Course in Applied Statistics*. Belmont, CA: Wadsworth, 1992.

Hawkins, Charles F. "Friendly Fire: Facts, Myths, and Misperceptions." *U.S. Naval Institute Proceedings*. June 1994: 54-59.

Kemp, Paul. *Friend or Foe, Friendly Fire at Sea 1939-1945*. London: Leo Cooper, 1995.

---. *U-boats Destroyed*. 1997. Annapolis: Naval Institute Press, 1997.

Niestlè, Axel. *German U-Boat Losses During World War II*. Annapolis: Naval Institute Press, 1998.

Potter, E. B., ed. *Sea Power: A Naval History*. Second ed. Annapolis: Naval Institute Press, 1981.

Roscoe, Theodore. *United States Destroyer Operations in World War II*. Annapolis: Naval Institute Press, 1953.

Ross, Sheldon M. *Introduction to Probability Models.*
Sixth ed. San Diego: Academic Press, 1997.

Troyka, Lynn Q. *Simon and Schuster Handbook for Writers.*
Englewood Cliffs, NJ: Prentice-Hall, 1987.

U.S. Naval and Shipbuilding Museum. *Dictionary of American
Naval Fighting Ships Online* (www.uss-salem.org/danfs).
1996.

U.S. Submarine Losses, World War II. 1946. Washington:
U.S. Government Printing Office, 1949.

United States Naval Chronology, World War II. Washington:
U.S. Government Printing Office, 1955.

INITIAL DISTRIBUTION LIST

1. Defense Technical Information Center 2
   8725 John J. Kingman Road, STE 0944
   Ft. Belvoir, Virginia 22060-6218

2. Dudley Knox Library 2
   Naval Postgraduate School
   411 Dyer Road
   Monterey, California 93943-5101

3. Wayne P. Hughes, Jr. 1
   Department of Operations Research (Code OR/HL)
   Naval Postgraduate School
   Monterey, California 93943-5101

4. James N. Eagle 1
   Department of Operations Research (Code OR/ER)
   Naval Postgraduate School
   Monterey, California 93943-5101

5. CNO Strategic Studies Group 2
   Naval War College
   Sims Hall
   686 Cushing Road
   Newport, Rhode Island 02841

6. Frank Uhlig 1
   Naval War College
   Code 35 Luce Hall
   686 Cushing Road
   Newport, Rhode Island 02841-1207

7. Charles Hawkins 1
   13140 Lakehill Drive
   Nokesville, Virginia 20181-3328

8. Christopher G. Blood 1
   Naval Health Research Center
   P.O. Box 85122
   San Diego, California 92186-5122

9.   Eugene P. Visco 1
     3752 Capulet Terrace
     Silver Spring, Maryland 20906

10. CDR Benjamin Yates 1
     200 Elizabeth Court
     Sterling, Virginia 20164-1930

11. Naval Historical Center 1
     Washington Naval Yard
     805 Kidder Breese SE
     Washington, District of Columbia 20374-5060

12. LT Lars R. Hagendorf-Orloff 3
     513 East Lincoln Avenue
     Royal Oak, Michigan 48067